Faulty Assumptions

Taking Custody of Your Classroom

William L. Miller

ROWMAN & LITTLEFIELD EDUCATION
A division of
ROWMAN & LITTLEFIELD PUBLISHERS, INC.
Lanham • New York • Toronto • Plymouth, UK

Published by Rowman & Littlefield Education
A division of Rowman & Littlefield Publishers, Inc.
A wholly owned subsidiary of The Rowman & Littlefield Publishing Group, Inc.
4501 Forbes Boulevard, Suite 200, Lanham, Maryland 20706
www.rowman.com

10 Thornbury Road, Plymouth PL6 7PP, United Kingdom

British Library Cataloguing in Publication Information Available

Library of Congress Cataloging-in-Publication Data

Miller, William L., 1949-
Faulty assumptions : taking custody of your classroom / William L. Miller.
p. cm.
Includes bibliographical references.
ISBN 978-1-61048-684-2 (cloth : alk. paper) -- ISBN 978-1-61048-685-9 (pbk. : alk. paper) -- ISBN 978-1-61048-686-6 (electronic)
1. Classroom management. I. Title.
LB3013.M555 2013
371.102'4--dc23

2013000366

The paper used in this publication meets the minimum requirements of American National Standard for Information Sciences Permanence of Paper for Printed Library Materials, ANSI/NISO Z39.48-1992.

Printed in the United States of America

Table of Contents

Preface

I've been around literally thousands of students in the last decade. One year alone, I was in seventeen different buildings. You see, I'm a substitute teacher or, as some prefer to call us, an emergency education specialist.

I'm certified K–12 and have been fortunate to work with students in every one of those grades. I've also taught in an alternative education school. I've been around bright kids and not-so-bright kids (that's PC for academically challenged). I've taught kids who have been in jail; kids who earned scholarships to MIT, Princeton, and Penn State; and every kind of kid in between. I've had arrogant kids, thoughtful kids, funny kids, go-getters, and kids with a "come and get me" attitude. And they all have two things in common: (1) not one of them likes to be ridiculed in front of their peers and (2) each and every one of them wants to feel important.

I've also discovered, to my chagrin, that some teachers, although well-meaning, can turn a bad situation into a calamity in short order. They have never learned to communicate effectively with students and so exert undo authority, or they have totally given up, watching the clock, looking forward to the final bell even more than their students do.

One young lady in a class of mine asked a question that's on most students' minds: "Why do I need this bull?" Upon hearing this, some teachers might go ballistic, pouring gasoline all over this small fire and turning it into a raging inferno in no time.

I, on the other hand, being there to not only teach but also further my research for this project, thought the question was right on target, if not thought-provoking. Most kids have no idea why they need to learn this stuff, because nobody has ever told them!

If you can't explain in one sentence why your course will have a positive impact on your students' lives, keep reading, because you need this bull!

This book explains in understandable terms why some students thumb their noses at a good education, disrupt everyone's day at every turn, and subject themselves to a lifetime of compromise and want. It is based on a decade of hands-on experience and research with students K–12, and in an alternative school setting. It explodes the accepted and timeworn theories to classroom management that are based on faulty assumptions, which rarely work and oftentimes make the situation worse.

It provides the practical answers that struggling teachers have been searching for to take custody of their classrooms in order to facilitate an educational environment conducive to good learning.

Written by a teacher for teachers, the principles advocated in these pages are applicable to all educators, veteran and novice, with any student, regardless of age.

OBSERVATIONS

- I'm not trying to be negative, I'm attempting to report some startling observations I've made over the years. I'm not trying to comfort, I'm trying to inform.
- Not talking about something usually causes far more problems than bringing everything out into the light of day and resolving it now.
- "There is no stigma attached to recognizing a bad decision in time to install a better one." —Laurence J. Peter, educator.

Acknowledgments

This book was a labor of love for me because I feel so passionate about ensuring every student has an opportunity to learn – even those who have not yet figured out that they do, in fact, want to learn and that education is their key to a brighter future.

I would like to thank Dr. Tom Koerner of Rowman and Littlefield who saw value in my research and gave me a chance to prove myself.

Dr. Cosmas Curry, who gave generously of his time, read a rough draft of *Faulty Assumptions*, and then asked to use it as a training manual for his faculty. It encouraged me to continue.

Robert O. Roberts, a lifetime educator, principal and superintendent who, after reviewing that same manuscript, called it "a breath of fresh air," encouraging me not to stop.

And Dr. Robert Gates, who liked what I was saying early on and invited me to speak each semester before the graduate students enrolled in classroom management and discipline classes of the Department of Education at Bloomsburg University of Pennsylvania.

Thanks to Dr. Steve Laidacker, a leading authority on "at risk" students, for graciously enduring my never- ending questions about this student population and allowing me to pick his brain over several months.

Plus the veteran public school and university educators, some I've only conversed with but never met, who provided the critical reviews needed to put *Faulty Assumptions* into a final draft. They include Mr. John Abell, Dr. Brian Toth, Mr. Michael Nailor, Dr. Barry Albertson, Dr. Gilbert Griffiths, as well as the aforementioned Dr. Curry and Mr. Roberts.

A big thank you also goes out to the hundreds of elementary and secondary teachers and administrators, college professors of education, those in the legal profession, and parents who shared their stories of joy and despair in dealing with students and kids of all ages. It led me to believe, without a doubt, that taking custody of your classroom is the most important aspect of the educational process, for without it, nothing else falls into place.

And a special thank you to writer and editor Patricia George for her patience and wisdom in helping put the finishing touches on a book I hope will change lives for the better.

But most importantly, I want to thank my partner through life Kay, who shared my frustration and my joy as we worked our way through the maze that is the publishing world until we came out on the other side, triumphant.

Chapter One

Attention Span of a Gnat

Picture a classroom full of energetic, loveable little hellions who, after the first minute of class (which in reality starts after three minutes of commotion), wish they were somewhere else. Anywhere else. You feel as though you have lost them before you've even gotten started—each one with the attention span of a gnat, right?

But truth be told, attention spans from one person to the next are about the same, give or take. Hey, teachers and students have something in common!

If you are in a movie theater and the flick is a stinker, what do you do? Yes, there are diehards who will gut it out because they already shelled out big bucks for the ticket, but if you are like most people, you get up and head for one of the exits.

Well, it's the same situation in your classroom. If a *lesson* is not engaging, students start looking for the exits—a way out. You may think your students are a captive audience; after all, you control the exit door. But students still find the escape route: inattention, indifference, and inappropriate behavior. The three *ins* of their *out*.

Why do people break out of jail? Because they don't want to be there! Picture yourself at your last in-service day and you'll get the picture.

After you have your class calm and attentive, a feat in itself, you have no more than one complete sweep of the second hand to establish how the entire class period will go. In that short time, your audience—and make no mistake about it, your students are your audience for the next forty-two minutes—will have made up their minds whether they are going to give you their time and attention or start looking for the exits.

Most of us have heard of the Golden Hour in medicine—the window of time after an injury during which treatment will likely prevent death. This is your *Golden Minute*. If you can't sell them something—actually *get them to buy into it*—in this Golden Minute, you will have an uphill climb all the way to the dismissal bell.

Some of you are saying, "I *rule* my classroom. I have no problems. My students know who is boss. If they don't toe the line, they know that their day is going to take a turn for the worse! I don't need this Golden Minute thing. They're mine all the way to the bell."

Are they really? Are you absolutely sure that the kid sitting in the back desk, the one you think is diligently hanging on your every word, is even in the same time zone as you are? Maybe he tuned you out as soon as you opened your mouth. Maybe she is smart enough to feign interest as her mind drifts toward the exit. Kids come to expect boredom in the classroom— whether actual or not, whether it is you, your subject, or both—and have adapted in order to survive. Flash back to in-service day for a reality check.

"But I'm not an entertainer," you say. Oh, yes you are. You may not be a *good* entertainer yet, but you are definitely an entertainer. And as much as you may want to deny it, your students are judging your performance every day. And they are hoping that this day will be different, that this forty-two- minute period won't feel like a week! They may be close to giving up hope. They may be headed for the exit.

It's time to reevaluate what goes on in your classroom. If your goal is to rule with an iron hand, you may consider your mission accomplished. If, on the other hand, you a want classroom full of young impressionable minds to open up to what you have to say, to truly want to learn, you must first capture their itty bitty, gnat-like attention spans in that Golden Minute. It sets the stage for the rest of the class period. Good or bad. Your choice.

~

OBSERVATIONS

- One way to avert a hostile takeover of a corporation is to make the acqui- sition as unattractive as possible. There's a lesson in here. When you have taken ownership of your classroom and have become a leader your stu- dents want to follow, the prospect of having other kids in the class take over the "corporation" becomes unattractive to everyone, including the corporate raiders, because it is no longer necessary and is counterproduc- tive.
- Real leadership creates the conditions ripe with opportunity for success and the means to accomplish it.
- The easiest way to reclaim your room is to never relinquish control to begin with.

- One teacher stands before a classroom full of impressionable minds and says, "Here I am." Another stands before the same students and says, "There you are." Guess who the students pay attention to?

Chapter Two

Your Objective Is What?

If you cannot define what your course is about and how it will matter to your students in real terms—real to *them*, that is—you need to think some more.

Why would you buy a car if its looks did nothing for you? Sure, it may be a good buy, but you will be cruising around in the thing for the next five to ten years. So you go back, rework your budget, and cough up a little more for a better-looking vehicle. Now you can live with yourself for the next decade.

Likewise, a student is not going to buy into a whole semester of your stuff if it has "bore fest" written all over it. And neither would you. Remember that dog of a movie at the theater? And remember the only exits your students have available to them? They'll use them, I guarantee it. Each day, each class period is the start of a brand-new movie, so you must grab those students in that Golden Minute so there is no mistake what your goal is for them that day. It can't be complicated. It must appear doable. And, if at all possible, it must seem enjoyable.

Some of you are rolling your eyes, shaking your heads, thinking, *I can't make my subject enjoyable!* There, you've finally admitted it to yourself, maybe for the first time. Your subject really may be boring.

"I can't put lipstick on this pig and pass it off as some type of video game at the mall," you say. Right you are. And wrong you are.

You are right because you have accepted the awful truth. Dangling participles and Latin language gone wild, while completely fascinating to you, simply do not appeal to a majority of your students. Put yourself in their place. Ask yourself, "Why *do* they need this bull?"

You are wrong if you think you can't pull it off. Most teachers are so protective of the precious subject they've conquered that they never view it from their students' vantage point. And that is where a lot of behavioral problems start. Your students believe that you know, deep down in your

5

heart, that this subject really sucks. But damn it, you just won't admit it! All they want is some signal from you that it's okay for them to apply the *suck* word to your subject because you feel their pain. This is hard to do, but it's a must if you want to keep discipline problems to a minimum. If you dare admit that your subject matter isn't always fascinating, you just might get an arm around the shoulder and a "hang in there; things will get better."

Now, how do you pull this off without them being any the wiser? How do you get them to start pulling for you? Good questions.

OBSERVATIONS

- If you don't learn something every day, you're wasting your time.
- The time to figure out the game plan is not in the middle of the game. If you want to avoid a clash that waits ahead, have a game plan in place before you get on the field.

Chapter Three

So You Know Your Student

Ask your head football, basketball, or lacrosse coach if he or she would go up against an opponent without having any knowledge of the opposing team's background, habits, tendencies, favorite plays, you name it. I bet you already know the answer.

Too often, teachers and students are strangers to each other. Oh sure, you know their names. You think you know something about them: background, family life, favorite band. But do you really *know* them? If called upon to write a one-page essay about ten random students, would you be able to do it? You think you could? What if your life depended on the accuracy of everything you wrote? Would you still be as confident?

What if you could use one of those lifelines from the TV game shows? Who would you call? The kids' parents? Friends? Your buddy, the teacher who had the students last semester? Last year? And how would you know that what they were telling you was accurate? Do you really want to rely on someone else's perception of these kids, knowing perceptions vary from person to person? Remember, it's your life at stake.

Surely you get my point. Or do you?

Mary had a girl in one of her classes who had been a behavior problem since the beginning of the year. So Mary sat down with the troubled teenager and, with an open, nonjudgmental attitude, had a heart to heart with her about what was fueling the girl's behavior. "She broke down and cried," Mary says. "The problems she was dealing with at home were totally overwhelming her. Since talking with me, her behavior has been much different."

Kids bring baggage to school each day—baggage that weighs them down so heavily that they end up dumping it all over you or anybody else in authority. It's almost therapeutic for some of them. Unfortunately, though, some teachers and administrators counter by dumping back on the student without taking the time to get to really know that student—his or her interests and how home life plays into all of this.

Any politician, comedian, or entertainer will tell you: if you don't know your audience, there's a good chance you're going to bomb. Remember that as we move on.

OBSERVATIONS

- Students will become more brazen and willing to challenge authority in direct proportion to the number of times they're allowed to get away with it.
- If you are a people person, people will forgive a lot of stupid things. Students are people.
- This is what I call a signature question. Ask any student: "If you had a spray can of paint, a bare wall, and nobody was looking, how would you tag it?" The answers will provide you with just about everything you need to know about a student, where his or her head is, and where to go from there.
- Some kids have so little confidence in their ability to reason they fear anything that requires a choice. If you put a chicken and a rabbit in front of them and ask them to point out the chicken, they'll scratch their heads and say, "I'm not real sure."

Chapter Four

Know Who You're Talking To

Respect is a funny thing. Teachers demand it; students crave it. The difference here is that as a teacher, you usually have it coming to you through your hard work, education, experience, and dedication to your profession.

Students just want it. No work, no effort, no nothing. "Just give it to me. I deserve it!" Some kids refer to this as getting their props, their proper respect. For some reason teachers can't get their props just by showing up, but students can!

How do you get a student to give you respect, your props? You can't, so stop trying. The behavioral problem, failing-in-school-type kid won't give you the time of day, let alone respect. So quit strutting around class trying to exchange props for props. It doesn't work that way. It never has.

The meet-me-halfway approach some teachers use to control classroom behavior is a recipe for disaster. Your classroom is not a democracy where majority rules. It is a benevolent dictatorship and you are the dictator. Consensus plays no part in classroom order and control. Comedian Bill Cosby, when asked his secret for success, said, "I don't know the secret of success. But I do know the secret of failure is trying to please everyone."

Read that quote from Dr. Cosby at least five times, *out loud*, until it sinks in. And then another five times. Engrave it in your mind.

In that Golden Minute, when a new class finally quits wiggling in their seats and you have what you think is their undivided attention (which you never really do, by the way), you have sixty seconds to establish—sell—your dictator role. And your students have one minute to buy it.

After your one-minute speech (which you have rehearsed, but it looks like it came off the top of your head . . . always very impressive), stop, look around the room slowly, and say, "Is that understood by everyone? Because if it's not, whoever did not get what I just made crystal clear may stay after class, and I'll go over it, word for word, personal-like. Anybody not get it? Raise your hand."

Nobody is going to stay after class to talk to you, but the potential pain-in-the-asses who plan to cause trouble throughout the semester *will* raise their hands. They'll self-identify. Now you know who they are! It's easier to deal with an adversary with a face. Now you can talk directly to the students who plan to wreak havoc in your class. These students, who love to play to an audience, really like this attention.

Remember, the key here is that you want them to give you the respect you deserve. And make no mistake about it, you do deserve it. And they know it. Make no mistake about that either. But they must want to give it to you. You can't just take it.

Now comes the tough part. They need a reason they can hang their hat on to give you that respect—even if it is grudgingly. You are in another Golden Minute.

Rehearsal time!

～

OBSERVATION

- When belligerent students form a mob, all hell can break loose very quickly. "We don't understand the rules. Write them down!" One senior spoke for the rest of our alternative education class one evening. Standing, I told them all, and especially this U.S. Navy–bound kid, "We have only one rule. Do as you're told! By the way, it is the same rule they have in the military!"
- When attempting to change unwanted behavior into acceptable behavior, remember this: they didn't get like this overnight, and they're not going to miraculously change overnight.

Chapter Five

Giving and Getting 100 Percent

How go your troublemakers, so goes your class.

More important, how goes your Golden Minute, so go the rest of the minutes. It sets up everything. That Golden Minute is the starting line in the 100-meter dash. If you come out of the blocks, eyes on the track, arms pumping, a clean, graceful start, you're on your way. If you look up too soon, stop pumping those arms, take a misstep, it's going to be a long race, and chances are you're not going to win. How's that for pressure?

Track stars practice their starts over and over until they can do them in their sleep. They know that the start sets up the rest of the race. It's crucial. It must be perfected. Yet too often, teachers, especially young new teachers, come out of the blocks way short of perfection. Consequently, the entire semester is an uphill race, a constant struggle to maintain order while trying to teach.

Teachers must achieve classroom order before they can be truly effective. Teachers can never achieve order with a fifty-fifty approach; with that they say, in effect, "You give me a little cooperation for a while, and I'll let you bend the rules for a little while. Okay?"

Is there a deal? Nope. Wrong approach. A truly effective classroom is not fifty-fifty; it's one hundred-one hundred. You give 100 percent effort; you fully expect them to give 100 percent. Period.

"How do I achieve that?" you ask. Begin at the beginning. Perfect your start.

A mother with two small children, a boy and a girl, maybe four and five years old, were in a store, and the children were completely out of control. They openly defied her at every turn. The mom was at her wit's end. She finally came up with a solution that she no doubt thought clever. She offered each child $2.00 to behave.

Did the kids take the money? Sure they did. It bought about a minute's peace. Then the kids were off to the races again. The woman, tears in her eyes, had to scoop up the kids, leave her unpurchased items on the counter with apologies to the clerk, and hurry out the door.

Who wouldn't feel sorry for her? She was miserable. But unfortunately she had brought it on herself. That problem never should have gotten that far.

You must address behavior problems *immediately*! The sooner you begin, the more respect students will maintain, and the more effective you will be. Let's keep this in mind as we continue to talk about your classroom and your teenagers.

～

OBSERVATIONS

- Wouldn't you just love to ask your "in-school dropouts" who can't wait to become the real thing, "If it's such a good idea, why isn't everyone doing it?"
- Life's not all that complicated. Either you want something and go after it or you sit back and think it's just going to happen.
- You're not stupid if you don't know something. You're only stupid if you *choose* to continue to not know.
- Goodness puts limits on kindness. There comes a time when you have to put your foot down and say, "This is wrong and I won't put up with it." There are some areas where kindness must give way to judgment. We must never confuse kindness with tolerance of improper behavior.
- There is a big difference between classroom leadership and classroom management. It's like the difference between effective and efficient. Doing something over and over again until you get it right is effective. Doing it right the first time is efficient. Leaders strive to get it right the first time. Leaders see what managers can't.
- When we dangle a GED like a carrot on the end of a stick, it entices far too many students who have the ability to earn a diploma but lack the motivation, or are just plain lazy, to shut down in school. Why make the effort to graduate when all one has to do is pass a lousy test?
- GEDs have their place. It affords those who, for whatever reason, did not follow through and get a diploma, and now see the light, an opportunity to correct their mistake. But GEDs must be viewed as a new beginning, not an end.
- "If I were hiring today, I would look for a particular thing, quite frankly. The thing I look for more than anything else is some evidence of determi-

nation, which I see is the most important quality in terms of how all people will do in their careers." —Businessman Mort Zuckerman

Chapter Six

Never Box Yourself In

Is that student you've been having problems with really the kid you think he is? Or is he the kid you've manufactured—with the help of your colleagues—in your mind? And why is it that some teachers take that same kid and have few or no problems?

Chances are that student who has been driving you nuts is not a problem with another teacher because: (1) the student has a healthy fear of that teacher, (2) the student has a healthy respect for that teacher, or (3) a combination of both. Behavior problems manifest themselves when relationships fall between the fear and respect factors.

A student who respects the teacher is never a chronic behavior problem. Never. And rarely is a student who fears a teacher being a constant disruption. Sure, a student may strike out at said teacher in some way, but it's usually to test for chinks in the teacher's armor.

Case in point: The director of an alternative education program, just by his sheer size and demeanor, could walk into a noisy room and freeze all students instantly with his gaze. His eye contact with a student was sufficient to straighten out anyone who needed straightening out. Rarely did he need to speak. But John's size or gaze of terror did not help him get to know the students. Nor did it compel the students to want to hear what he had to say. His temporary victory was based on a sense of terror, not respect.

The "scaring the bejeebers out of them" game plan rarely accomplishes anything other than a momentary ceasefire. Where do you go from there? Students who respect you—whether they *like* you or not—are students you can mold.

Never let your own behavior as a teacher box you in and leave you in a bad place. Keep in mind that problem students have a way of multiplying!

Your goal is not to punish or humiliate but to change poor student behavior into acceptable behavior. Leave yourself options.

OBSERVATIONS

- The brain's frontal lobe, which controls (among other things) decision making, is the last to fully mature. This occurs around twenty-six years. And until it gets all wired up proper-like, you may be fighting a losing battle with some of these kids.
- Some students are treading water and running short of air. There is always a reason for poor behavior and lackadaisical effort. Someone, maybe you, needs to sit down with this kid and say, "You're too good a person for us to continue this way." Nobody gains anything by turning a blind eye to the obvious.
- Don't judge a situation until you understand it. You want to resolve the situation, not entangle it.

Chapter Seven

How to Find the Right Approach

People do things for one of two reasons: because they want something to happen or because they want something *not* to happen. If you know your students, you will know their motivation. But you must really know your students. Do you?

You're saying to yourself, "There he goes again. I don't *want* to get to know them. And neither would you! I teach; they listen. That's my game plan." Great. If it's working, don't change. Write a book about it! Dig in your heels. Don't budge. But let me clue you in on a little secret: the better you know your students, the better they behave.

Consider this basic rule: *if you can't fix it, don't make it worse.* In other words, first, do no harm. Of course, the better you know your students and the better they know you, the easier it is to apply this principle. Consider this:

In baseball, when you have a runner caught between second and third base, and the pitcher has the ball, the best thing for the pitcher to do is run directly at the runner, thereby forcing the runner to make a choice: continue to third or try to make it back to second. If the runner tries to advance to third, the pitcher should throw the ball to the third baseman, who then runs the runner back to second and tries to make the play there. Why? If you get the runner out, great! If he makes it back to second safely, you haven't lost anything. He's right back where he started and happy to be there.

If what you try in order to turn unwanted behavior into acceptable behavior does not work, will it make the situation go south? Will it set you back? Will it make the situation worse? If the answer is "probably not," then try it! You must always leave yourself the option to try something else.

Unwanted behavior can take many forms, from chronic tardiness and late assignments to daily disruption so massive that you just want that student out of your class. Bad behavior can also take a subtle form that, if left unchecked, can spiral out of control, eventually affecting all your students negatively. Remember, there is always a reason behind the behavior. Discover what that reason is, and you are halfway home.

Case in point: Ally chose a subtle form of misbehavior to bolster her standing with her peers. How the teacher dealt with her fairly innocuous grab for power illustrates how you can apply that cardinal rule: *if you can't fix it, don't make it worse.*

This senior girl took it upon herself to start addressing the teacher as Bill instead of Mr. Miller. At first she did that only when addressing him one-on-one. Then she began addressing him by his first name in front of her classmates. The teacher hoped she would realize all by herself that this was not a good idea, but she just got bolder. It was time for a course correction.

The only thing the teacher knew for sure was this: disruptive behavior *always* fills a need. It's helpful to discover what that need is, but it's not always necessary. He asked her to stay after class one day—remember, never correct students in front of their peers—and said, "Do you think it's appropriate for a student to address a teacher by his first name?" (And remember, after you ask a question, shut up and listen. The student's answer, or lack of one, will tell you where to go from there.)

Ally stared at him, probably expecting a verbal barrage. But he said nothing else. He just stared back.

"No," she replied meekly.

"I was just wondering. See you later," the teacher said.

When correcting students, all students, no matter what the offense, it's *always* best to give them the opportunity to correct themselves. It then becomes their idea, not yours! If the teacher had flown off the handle and unleashed the verbal barrage she was most likely expecting, this girl would have shut down with him and perhaps become a worse problem in class.

(By the way, she always addressed him as Mr. Miller after that. And the whole thing involved only twenty-four spoken words between the two of them, and less than thirty seconds.)

If you get to know your students, will it hurt your attempts to control classroom behavior? Probably not. It actually may help.

Case in point: Bethany was a sophomore and quite a hell-raiser: talkative, rarely paid attention, disruptive, etc. She had a sub, Mr. Johnson, in her social studies class for two days. The regular teacher, Mr. Smith, was known to run a tight ship, but the sub wasn't sure what to expect.

The first day was pretty much a wash. Mr. Johnson got through the lesson plans okay. The kids did their work. But there was the usual disregard for rules that's commonplace when students see a sub walk in the door. Sure, they said, Mr. Smith let them sit wherever they wanted (despite the fact he had left a seating chart). Really, Mr. Smith did let them listen to their iPods during class. Mr. Johnson wasn't about to put up with their foolishness again the second day. A few minutes before the bell at the end of class on that first day, he stood up, walked around the teacher's desk, and sat on top of it. He held a paper on which he had scribbled a few names. The class froze, wondering why he had suddenly come to life. They probably were more curious than anything else.

Slowly, he said in a deep, monotone voice, "Mr. Smith informed me before he left that this class was his problem class." He pointed his finger slowly in a sweeping motion around the room. "He said I should take names."

He lifted the paper and turned it toward them so they could see that he had written down 12 or so names. He knew they couldn't actually read the list because of the distance and the fact that even he couldn't read his own handwriting.

"I'll be here again tomorrow. I'll bring this piece of paper with me. Anyone who pulls another performance like today's will get a check next to their name. That will mean that for two days in a row you chose to act like knuckleheads. Mr. Smith wants to see this paper upon his return. He assured me if anyone acted up in class, heads would roll. I'll let you interpret what he means by that. Have a nice day. See you tomorrow."

The next day, he purposely stayed in the hall for a full minute past the tardy bell. He wanted to make a grand entrance. He sat down behind the desk, took out the paper with the names from the previous day so all could see, and perused the list, glancing up now and then, as if to make sure *that* student was in attendance. Truth be told, he didn't know one student from another. The names on the list were there at random from the grade book. The only one he knew for sure was Bethany, and only because Mr. Smith had forewarned him.

Halfway through the class, which was going smoothly, Bethany made her way up to his desk and whispered, "Mr. Johnson, is my name on that list?"

Mr. Johnson just smiled and said, "What do you think?"

"Yeah," she said.

He decided to go a bit further. "Bethany," he said as he looked over the list, "your name is at the top of the list." Dejectedly, she went back to her seat. He could see by her sad expression that she couldn't afford to get in any more trouble, especially with Mr. Smith.

At the end of class, which had gone so smoothly he wished he had it on video, he got the students' attention. He took the paper with the names and held it up. "Mr. Smith asked for a list." He paused for effect.

"Bethany, would you come here please?" She stood in front of the desk, not knowing what was coming.

"You've all been really good today. I appreciate that. It's hard for a sub sometimes."

He took the paper, crumbled it up, handed it to Bethany, and said, "Would you put that in the garbage can for me?" A huge smile lit her face as she took the paper.

"If you don't tell Mr. Smith, I won't," he said as she walked over to the can. Relieved laughter and applause filled the room.

Most of those students never gave him a problem again. And Bethany? She was his pal from then on. She always said, "Good morning, Mr. Johnson," whenever he was in school. She grew up before his eyes, probably just through the course of normal maturation, but he likes to think he had something to do with it! The last time he saw her was in a Wal-Mart. She ran up to him and asked, "Mr. Johnson, do you remember me?" Of course he did. He said, "Sure I do, Bethany. It's good to see you. What have you been up to?" That talkative, disruptive tenth grader was a sophomore in college. Time flies!

OBSERVATIONS

- Life involves successes and failures. It's how we handle both that shows us, and the rest of the world, who we are. Of these two, failure may be the more alluring, simply because it not only reflects our character but also offers an opportunity to learn and grow as human beings.
- Point out to your students who use bad luck and poverty as a crutch for their lot in life that those things have little to do with holding them back. It's almost always their poor choices.
- Kid, you want a reason to try hard? If you fail, you look stupid. If you succeed, you make everyone who was sure you couldn't succeed look stupid.
- If love is all it took, we would have no more behavior problems.
- Truth be told, you really can't be anything you want to be. That's a myth. You can only aspire to be anything you want to be. Without the drive and determination and the willingness to sacrifice something now to become that person, it just isn't going to happen.
- Who we are is based on the accumulation of our choices.
- Dropping out is a lot like smoking. You don't know when it will make you sick, but it will.

Chapter Eight

What Are You Trying to Accomplish?

Whatever you try to do to solve a problem must not set you back. It must not hurt what you are trying to accomplish. If what the sub had tried with Bethany didn't work, could he have tried something else? Of course he could. And what he did do didn't make the situation worse. If he had yelled and screamed and threatened to send one and all to the principal's office, then found to his horror that that wasn't working, could he go back and try what he tried? No.

If you can't fix the problem, don't make it worse! He didn't threaten. He didn't make demands. He allowed the students to make a choice based on the information he supplied them. Then he sat back to see what would happen. He knew that with what he was trying, it couldn't get worse. And that was his goal. Sure, he played a little fast and loose with the truth. But he calls that "improving on the truth."

Most of those students never caused any real problem again. In their young eyes he was a decent guy, okay in their book. He could become a jerk later on. But if he was a jerk from the get-go, he couldn't then become an okay guy. Get it? *If it does not help, it must not hurt your cause.* The students did not want to get in trouble with Mr. Smith. The first day's misbehavior pretty much assured that they were already in trouble. Now, to what degree of trouble had yet to be established. But they made a decision that they didn't want to compound that trouble with two straight days of bad conduct. That would be worse, much worse. They *needed* to behave. They *wanted* to behave. He simply gave them the means and opportunity to do so.

Remember the golden rule, that Golden Minute. In each class, you will learn quickly which students are problem students and which are cut-ups. Which students have the potential to disrupt your class on a consistent basis and which students are just acting their age and seeing how far they can push the envelope. There is a difference, and you must quickly determine which is which. Some kids are just being lovable little goofballs and some are hell bent on causing you as many problems as possible. Disruption is their game. It's their way of getting attention at any cost.

There are many reasons these students seek and desperately need attention. And often, they don't care about the consequences. A trip to the principal's office just feeds their attention-fetching ways. So how do you stop, or at least contain, these kids and their disruptive behavior?

Good question. And you must come up with an answer early on, or you will be perceived as weak, indecisive, and not in control of your classroom. And if *you* are not in control, guess who is?

Take a look at parents who have lost control of their households to these teenage terrors. Sometimes these parents have taken the path of least resistance because they are young, maybe single moms or dads, and inexperienced, having discovered parenting is not as easy as it looks. Or the parents are veterans who are just plain tired. And, having tried everything they could think of to regain control of their households (oftentimes making matters worse), they throw in the towel simply because they are so overwhelmed and are worn out from fighting. At that point, they have abdicated their responsibly as authority figures in order to get just a little perceived peace under their roofs. Take a look around your room. Guess what? These tiny terrors are now dotting your classroom. The parent's or guardian's problems are now your problems.

A clever paper was tacked to a bulletin board in the faculty room. It was about a parent calling their child's school and getting those annoying instructions as to which number to push to get the correct party:

> Press 1 if you would like a new teacher for your child because the current one is so unfair.
> Press 2 if you would like to discuss your child's failing grade on her most recent term paper, which you actually wrote.
> Press 3 if you would like us to raise your child.

Many of the parents you'll be dealing with *have* pressed 3. It's convenient. It's even reasonable, at least to them. And it allows plausible deniability. "I pushed the wrong button!"

To deal effectively with students, you'll have to know the following: (1) from whence they came, (2) what the student wants, (3) what you want, and (4) how to marry all three. It can be complex. Every case is different. But it's doable.

OBSERVATIONS

- "The greatest discovery of any generation is that a human being can alter his life by altering his attitude." — William James, American psychologist and philosopher
- We are not being friends to students by negotiating with them.
- When you allow these kids to continue their defiance and disrespect, does anyone really believe it helps them?
- Good behavior should not be rewarded. You don't reward someone for doing what they should be doing in the first place. It's expected. Continual good behavior is rewarded with added privileges and added responsibilities, which lead to more privileges. This introduces the concept to some of these kids, many for the first time, that productive behavior is far more rewarding, far less stressful, and possibly far more lucrative down the road. It's how it plays in the real world. Now you're preparing them to carry on without us.
- We fall short in preparing students for what might and might not happen. Therefore, they have no concept of what to expect in real life down the road. This is what teaching to the test has gotten us.
- "We can't afford to have a country of just over 300 million people, with a third of our people uneducated, under educated, unskilled, and unable to access the economy of today and tomorrow being ticked off and becoming wards of the state. That's not going to work. This system has to change. And the people who are defending the status quo have got the interest of the adults instead of the interests of our children and the future of our country." — Tim Pawlenty, former Minnesota governor, in a May 2011 interview on "This Week with Christiane Amanpour"
- When we teach our children that every time something happens to them that they don't like they are victims, we further erode their ability to function in the real world.

Chapter Nine

Who's Listening

Once upon a time, many lifetimes ago, I sold life insurance. It was absolute torture for me to take in hand the list of prospective clients—all total strangers—and attempt to set up appointments to sell them something they didn't really want. I was never sure what was more tortuous: talking to people I knew nothing about or attempting to sell them something they would try to reject. It was an awful uphill struggle for me.

Do you as a teacher sometimes have those same feelings? Are there some students who absolutely drive you nuts? Of course there are. You would be the rare exception if you said no. They are part of every school: little creatures foisted upon you by an unforgiving administration and clueless parents, just to make sure your day never goes smoothly. And do you really know who these pains are? Sure, you know their names. You look hopefully each morning to see if they are listed on the absentee sheet!

Let's get back to the insurance analogy for a second. It's true that the more you know about the prospective buyer, the more insurance you sell. Knowledge of your buyer opens more doors to exploit—yes, exploit. It's the same with students. The more student info you have in your arsenal, the more likely you are to survive a forty-two-minute period that should be enjoyable for both you and your students, but at times feels like you have been through a forty-two-minute battle for control of your room. Not only survive, but also thrive. You need to come into the classroom loaded for bear. And the way you load up for bear—the student who is driving you over the edge—is with as much info as you can obtain about this kid.

Perhaps you've heard this maxim: "If we can just sit down and talk, we'll find we're not that far apart. We have a lot in common."

"Hey, I'm not going to do that," you say. "Not with this punk. No way!"

That can be true—to a point. But you need to ask yourself an important question: "Do I want to keep butting heads with this kid all semester?" If your answer is yes, quit reading and go directly to the next chapter. If you're still with me, let me elaborate.

Any kid you are constantly butting heads with is constantly butting heads with other people, too. You're not someone special he or she has zeroed in on. It's a pattern. A learned pattern. And what's the one thing you and I and every other butthead have in common with this kid? We all want to feel important! It's as natural a craving as breathing. As natural as making sure your best side is facing the camera. And if making lives miserable is what it takes to feel important, they're willing to do it. Oftentimes it's the only way they know to express themselves. It says, "I'm here. I need attention and right now, too. I'm in charge and you're not."

Look around at the faces in your classroom the next time the class clown takes over and try to tell me I'm wrong. To feel important, to get that desperately needed and wanted attention, they need an eager audience. Think how often you have felt the young eyes of the audience on you, waiting to see how you'll react, secretly hoping there'll be an explosion.

Put yourself in the class clown's shoes, too. Rebelling against authority with virtually no consequences? Not in this day and age. They want an explosion? Mission accomplished. The kid won, again. He got the whole class's attention and topped it all off by triggering Mt. Vesuvius!

How's that for making the kid feel important and the center of attention? If you took away his audience—imagine just the two of you in the room— chances are he wouldn't pull this nonsense. And I'm quite sure you wouldn't lose control either. That has got to tell you something. *If you want to put out a fire, take away what's fueling it.* If you want to turn it into a raging inferno, pour gasoline on it.

Case in point: A fellow teacher, Alex, was working with me in alternative education one evening. He came to work in a foul mood. I had no idea what caused his bad attitude, but he definitely was not his usual self.

In the class that night was a habitual behavior problem kid who irked the hell out of Alex just by being there. The kid knew it, even took delight in it. Truth be told, this kid had this uncanny ability to push just the right buttons on just about any teacher. Kaboom! It was great sport for him. He was what I referred to as a lifer: in and out of alternative education. Mostly in. But a likeable kid with potential. (And I'll talk about that later. It's that important.)

Alex told this kid to do something (it doesn't matter what). The kid said he wouldn't, he didn't like the way Alex talked to him, and Alex couldn't make him. You can see where this was going. Alex blew! He was all over the kid in a flash. The rest of the students stopped what they were doing to watch. Voila! Instant captive audience.

A small fire was about to turn into a raging inferno. If you have never had the privilege of working with a whole room full of chronic-behavior-problem kids, understand that something innocuous can escalate into an all-out war in no time. And it can have lasting effects on the whole group.

Remember, whatever you chose to do in any situation, *if you can't fix it, don't make it worse.* You must leave yourself the option to try something else.

Trying to head off the inferno, I walked over to Alex and whispered in his ear, "I think I know what's causing this kid to act like this tonight. Do you mind if I have a minute with him?"

To my relief Alex said, "Go ahead."

I had followed my cardinal rule. I would not do something that could make matters worse. And I could always try something else if my whispered words had fallen on deaf ears. If I had said, so everyone could hear, "Mr. Black, you should know better that this!" or, "Mr. Black, you need to chill!" and it didn't work, could I have then whispered my offer to take over and gotten the result I wanted? No! Alex would have become defensive, gotten pissed off at me for interfering, and there would have been a really big explosion.

Instead I was quiet, I asked Alex's permission, and I implied that the kid was at fault and that Alex was justified. Alex left the room, which was my goal. I then sat down next to this kid, who was itching for a confrontation.

"Tim, would you mind telling me what's going on?" I asked quietly. I wasn't judgmental. I asked for his side. *And* I made a point to get to know this kid. One of Tim's hang-ups was he thought everyone was dissing him all the time. He wanted his props (proper respect).

"Mr. Black is always on my case."

"Why do you think that is?" I asked.

I was not judgmental. I continued to speak quietly. I asked his opinion. I tried to defuse the anger. Time will always be on your side as long as you do nothing to escalate the problem. The old "count to ten and take a deep breath" actually works. Remember: if you get loud, the kid gets louder. If you get hostile, the kid gets more hostile. If you remain calm, the kid usually becomes calmer. And the only way you're going to get anywhere in this situation is with *calm.*

As I said, I knew who I was dealing with. Tim's mother was not a supportive parent. She was anti-teacher, anti-authority. She thought she was better than everyone else, and she passed this attitude on to her son. "Don't take any bunk from those teachers!" I could just hear her saying. I had seen her in action before. It never occurred to her that she might be the reason her fifteen-year-old was bounced out of school after school.

I knew Tim's background and had taken an educated guess at what was going on that day. I waited for an answer to my question. Waited! When you ask a question, shut up, even if it kills you to do so. If the kid is thinking of an answer to your question, he's probably not thinking of another way to misbehave, at least for the moment. What seems like an eternity is really ten to fifteen seconds, max.

Finally, Tim responded calmly. "I'm having a bad day. Mr. Black didn't do anything wrong."

"When he comes back in here, if you apologize, I bet that will be the end of it. What do you say?"

"Okay."

Situation diffused. And Tim did apologize. He did so in a way that allowed him to save face, which is so important to these kids.

Know as much as you can about your students, *especially* your problem students. I promise you, it will come in handy.

~

OBSERVATIONS

- There is very little training in school that prepares students for life on the street. Columnist Ann Coulter may have said it best. "Reality betrays children constantly."
- All students, when they begin their school years, have a certain seriousness about the desire to learn from and please those in charge of that learning. At some point, far too many of these former scholars become nonserious people, just passing through.
- All students, especially "at risk" kids, need consistency and structure. Take a look at your alternative education program, or whatever passes for one, and ask yourself honestly if these two vital ingredients are there. If not, start to rethink the whole thing. You decide what must be done that day, not the students!

Chapter Ten

What's It Going to Take?

No matter what you do in your classroom, you're going to run into some trouble. Your goal is to reduce that trouble to a manageable level. You do this by knowing each student. If you don't know your student, you'll have no idea what approach will work with him, what will get through to him on his level. Some kids need a pat on the back to get them started in the right direction; some kids need a kick in the butt. You've got to know *when* to pat 'em on the head and *when* to kick 'em in the butt.

It's a learned art that comes with time and experience. But whether you're an old hand or new to the business, I can assure you, if you don't get to know your students—their interests, their likes and dislikes, what turns them on and what turns them off—you're going to run into trouble.

There's an old adage that says, *If you know yourself but don't know your enemy, there is danger in one hundred battles. If you know your enemy but don't know yourself, there is danger in one hundred battles. But if you* know *yourself and* know *your enemy, there is no danger in those one hundred battles.*

A one-size approach does not fit all. Size 8AA shoes will fit some people. Some will flop around in them and some will have their toes pinched so hard they'll throw them off the first chance they get. And yet, some teachers use the one-size-fits-all approach to discipline. They are shocked—shocked, mind you—to learn that some kids rebel against what other kids accept.

Let's agree on one thing from here on out: discipline begins to take care of itself when students find learning meaningful. This is when motivation takes root and a student's ambition kicks in. *Motivation* is something some of these kids sorely lack. Remember the two reasons people (students) do something: *they want something to happen or they want something not to happen.*

29

A lack of motivation or lack of desire to learn is one of the root causes of behavior problems in school. Kids place little value on education, thinking, *I've gotten by without it so far just fine, thank you.* A poorly motivated student is trouble waiting to happen. Idle hands do the devil's work. That sort of thing.

Kyle, a twenty-year-old student who had been out of school for more than two years, was disruptive and, by his own admission, a real jerk in school. Drugs and alcohol played a role in his decision to drop out of school, but the birth of a son when he was nineteen had started the process of what I call *the Shock Point.*

That's the point when someone's vision of how the world works collides with how the world really works. It's the process that everyone goes through at some point in their young lives when they discover to their horror that they really don't have all the answers. Hell, they don't have any answers! Now all the screwing around in school comes back to haunt them. It ain't fun no more.

Kyle was one of our best students, never a problem in our alternative education school. Focused. Dedicated. *Motivated* to make up for lost time. We didn't need to motivate him to earn his high school diploma. The shock of living in the real world without one had done that just fine.

If you could have access to a time machine, wouldn't it be great if you could strap in your behavior-challenged students for a ride five years into the future, drop them off for a year on their own in the real world, and then bring them back? Your classroom discipline would improve dramatically. Since that is not possible yet, you'll have to improvise. And it starts with knowing your student enough to know what it's going to take.

~

OBSERVATIONS

- Why is the yardstick some kids use to measure other kids they want to be like too often measuring the "not going anywhere and getting there fast" students?
- Some behavior-problem kids have a basic need to mold reality to their beliefs. This rationalization is quite comforting. When you think you have something figured out, there is a sense of relief.
- Truth is the first casualty of war. See above.
- When you pay people not to work, you are going to get a whole lot of people who don't want to work. When you reward a student for misbehaving in school (when you don't do anything constructive about it) you are going to get a whole lot of misbehaving in school. This is not hard to

figure out. And yet, some otherwise fairly logical people struggle mightily with this simple concept.

- Every student you call in for a correction, a sit down, needs to walk away from that meeting refreshed with a better understanding and a new appreciation of you and your work.

Chapter Eleven

Are You Positive?

Did you ever open a class with some brilliant oratory you practiced over and over in your head until it was perfect, only to have to repeat it because half your students' minds were somewhere else? We all have. It's frustrating. And the repeat performance always lacks the pizzazz of the original. It's never as good. It loses its *oomph*. Your timing is off, and timing is extremely important.

Bill stood in front of his desk, wristwatch in hand, looking around at an unruly class, then periodically back to his watch, then back at the class. This went on for a little more than two minutes. When the class finally quieted itself, he just shook his head and said quietly, but making sure all could hear, "Not good. Not good at all." He had their attention, but the way he it got was negative. He implied that heads were going to roll next time. And getting attention in a negative way can *never* compete with getting attention in a positive way.

Remember, we do stuff because we *want something to happen or we want something not to happen.* Bill had definitely implied that their behavior was unacceptable. And it was. But now he had to turn a negative into a positive. The class got off on the wrong foot. They knew it. And now they were on guard.

If Bill had instead written on the board, "Attention third period. Anyone who is in their seat and quiet when the bell rings will get a jumbo candy bar," voila! He would have had everyone's attention. Not because they didn't want something to happen, but because they did. Big difference.

Positive always trumps negative. Both will get their attention, but you don't want to be standing in front of your desk, holding your watch the entire period!

If the watch watching hadn't worked, could Bill have tried something else? Could he have screamed and hollered later? Sure. If he screamed and hollered first, could he have gone all nice later? Sure. But the mood would have been set. Negative would have ruled the next forty-two minutes.

Now consider if he had written on the board, "Attention, third period. I will give everyone a jumbo candy bar, if *every* student is quiet and in their seat at the bell." He would then have an army of students in his corner quieting the class for him.

To get the attention you *want*, you must talk in terms of what the other guy wants. That goes for entire classes as well as individuals. With the candy bar example, you wouldn't even have to speak. You Golden Minute would be on the board. It's concise. The terms are explicit. You would get every- one's attention because it spoke to something that appealed to everyone.

This is important when dealing with an individual problem student also. It is important for that student to have something to shoot for, something he or she not only wants but also sees as *achievable*.

And here's the most important part: it must be quickly attainable. To buy into whatever you've chosen to motivate them out of their poor behavior, they must see success early on. They can't see five years down the road. In reality, they can't see past the last bell.

Use tiny steps for even your toughest problem. Inch by inch. That sort of thing. You must make it seem doable and, if possible, enjoyable. For that to happen, you must snag them on a dream . . . something they want but may not even know it yet or something they think is beyond their grasp.

I once asked a class, "What is the one thing you would like to do in your life if I could absolutely guarantee that you'd be successful? There would be absolutely no chance you'd fail. I'd see to it." The class was silent. I looked around the room at each problem kid, looking for reactions. Anything. No one had ever made them such an offer. Then I could see in their eyes a sudden glimmer of hope.

"Take that one thing you're thinking about right now, and write it down on a piece of paper. Don't show anyone else what it is. Go."

Every one of my students took out a piece of paper and jotted something down. It was gratifying. It said to me that, yes, even those kids who had given up hope, those whose only way to get the attention they craved was through disruption and poor behavior, had something that was important to them.

I now had my "in." Papers in hand, I now had an opportunity to personal- ize my Golden Minute to each individual student.

To capture an entire class's attention, or anyone's, you must speak in terms of what they want. It must appear doable. It must appear achievable. And *you* must be, in their young eyes, an integral part of that process.

OBSERVATIONS

- "The only real power is the power to persuade the people." —Richard Newstat, political scientist
- The satisfaction in accomplishment brought about by one's own effort and drive, in falling down and picking oneself back up, cannot be glossed over. And yet, in our hurry to rush some students through this education thing and push them out the door, as if they had a "use by" date stamped on them, we rob them of any opportunity to experience life's ups and downs. We take from them real-world learning when we hold their hands tight so they don't fall.
- When you change your attitude, you get to do something different.
- "Education is what remains after one has forgotten everything he learned in school." —Albert Einstein

Chapter Twelve

What Do They Want?

All students need and crave attention, although few will admit it. Even those shrinking violets in the back of the room you are absolutely sure will shun the spotlight for the rest of their lives crave attention.

Think about it. When you look at a group photograph, whose face do you look for first? Your own, right? Don't deny it. It's human nature. It's okay. When kids look at a photo, when they pick out their clothes, when they see their name in the paper—they say to themselves, "There *I* am!"

We all think in terms of ourselves; our students even more so. Now let's say the president of the United States strolled unexpectedly into your classroom, spotted that shy wallflower in your class, and said, "Young lady, I'd like to shake your hand. I've been told by many people that you do outstanding work in this school." What do you think would happen? Would she freeze up? Maybe. That's understandable. But I'm quite sure she would be beaming inside. She would love that attention, especially because the whole class was watching.

Let's rewind. Suppose *before* the president arrived, you told the shy violet he was coming tomorrow and was eager to meet her. Do you think she would skip school? Not likely. Every student has something, a trigger if you will, that causes the brain to click into focus. Whether shrinking violet or master of disruption, each has particular motivators.

Learn all you can about *each* of your students. Keep a file if necessary. Remember, people do things for two reasons only: *they want something to happen, or they want something not to happen.* Of the two, the first is by far the most motivating.

And yet, a lot of teachers use as their only so-called motivating tool, the "I'm in charge and you are not" thing. Nothing clicks into focus with that. You see, to learn something new, everyone needs a reason to latch onto it.

And whether you agree or not, students deserve an explanation why whatever you are teaching is, or will be, important to them. It may be your job to sell your subject matter, but first you must be sure they are willing to buy.

What's more, students must not only buy into what you're selling but also buy into the seller. That's you! You are more important than your subject! Until a student feels comfortable with you, trusts in, believes in, and accepts you as a genuine good guy, you're climbing uphill with your problem students. There is no replacing a good salesman, no matter how great the product being sold.

The cardinal rule in sales is you must talk in terms of what the other guy wants or needs. And sometimes they don't even know what they want or need until you point it out to them. For example, a new home buyer may never have thought of the advantages of a sun room. With the windows open, what a pleasure it can be on a summer evening! If positioned right, it may even heat itself on a sunny, winter day. Here's the visual: a hot cup of coffee on a crisp Sunday morning in the sun room, all toasty and warm as snowflakes fall then melt on the window glass. The buyer is sold on something she never considered before. Screw the cost. There's a sale because she can visualize that Sunday morning.

Visualization is an effective tool when you're trying to get someone's undivided attention. And for problem kids to want to listen to what you have to say, you have to talk in terms of what they want or need. Remember, they usually don't see the possibilities for their future until you point them out. Help them start visualizing.

Ask a problem student what he sees himself doing five years down the line. Most times you'll get a blank expression and a shoulder shrug. They can't see past three o'clock, let alone five years down the road. Experience is life's greatest teacher and we must not forget that experience is exactly what our students lack. Since seeing their future is not one of their strong suits, you'll have to get them started. How do you help someone who is anti-school, anti-education, pro-disruption see far enough into their future to change their ways, and do it in short order?

It ain't easy. But it can be done. And visualization is the key.

~

OBSERVATIONS

- Most attention-getting behavior is the byproduct of insecurity. It says, "Here I am. Pay attention to me instead of the teacher." Reduce the insecurity, and you reduce the attention-getting ways.

- Teens need a coherent strategy to succeed in our ever-changing and competitive world. Ask your more disruptive students what their strategy is. The answer should give you valuable insight into why they behave as they do.
- Some kids are smarter than other kids for the simplest reason: they put in the time to get smarter. They knew one of these days they would be further down the road and it would probably come in handy.
- In this country, you will be given every opportunity to succeed, to become anyone you aspire to be. When you quit school, you give that up.
- Fear of failure is an albatross that holds even the brightest back.

Chapter Thirteen

You, Them, Together

What now?

Good question. How can you sell yourself and your content? How can you convince your problem students that it is in their best interest to apply themselves in your class? They haven't done it so far, so why would they start now? Why would they change from doing something they are very good at—driving you nuts—to being cooperative?

All kids are different. Some actually *want* to change. They know their behavior isn't getting them anywhere. But change is difficult. With change, one must give up something to become something else. Some kids will vehemently resist change simply because change frightens them. They have honed their persona. It's who they are.

Case in point: Bobbi was fifteen, an alternative-education student who had perfected her bad-girl image. She could piss off a teacher (her main target) with little effort and then drive the nails in with exact precision. She was a genius when it came to being the baddest female in class.

And if you knew her background, you'd probably understand, even appreciate her behavior. When both parents were incarcerated for drugs, Bobbi was shipped off to a foster family. She once told me she was there when a drug deal had gone bad in her own home. She came to the assistance of her drug-dealing dad when he was getting the worst of it by slamming his customer over and over again with a baseball bat. She was nine years old at the time. The pain and anger were clearly in her eyes six years later.

Yet, incredibly, that wasn't what this young girl was most embarrassed about. It dawned on me during a current events discussion in class. I began asking questions about the history of one of the topics. Bobbi took charge, answering every question with accuracy and confidence. It became a game as to whether I could stump her. I couldn't. It was a side of this girl I had never seen before. She was brilliant!

And the game would have continued had Bobbi not felt the gaze of every other student in the class on her, startled expressions on their faces. *Who* was this? You could almost hear the other behavior-problem students asking themselves this question. This was not the bad girl they had come to admire. Bobbi stopped on a dime and didn't say another word. I realized in that moment that she was actually embarrassed by how smart she was.

Nice story, you say. So what does this have to do with classroom behavior? Everything! This girl was obviously interested in world events. I now had my in with her. She was also smart. Another useful bit of information. She unwittingly supplied me with ammo and allowed me to correct the direction of how I would deal with her. With my newfound knowledge, I could relate any subject in school to her likes and make it relevant to her young life. I now had my "in" to show her how it would be to her advantage to buckle down—if only for forty-two minutes a day—and learn, as best *we* could, my subject.

A focused student is a better-behaved student. A better-behaved student is a more teachable student. A more teachable student is a more successful student. And success breeds success. But before you can try to win a student like Bobbi over to your way of thinking, you must be absolutely sure you can relate your subject to her interests, her wants, and her likes and dislikes. Relate it to *her*. When the time comes, you'll have one minute, yes, that one Golden Minute, to win her over (at least get her to lean in the right direction) or blow the opportunity.

Start practicing your sales pitch, but remember one important thing: if you can't convince yourself about the importance of knowing your subject, you're not going to convince a teenager. What meaning does your subject have for these kids? Start your spiel.

∽

OBSERVATIONS

- Students: these four years in high school are not yours to keep. You only get to lease them. The only thing you get to keep and take with you for the rest of your life is what you get out of them. Good or bad. Your choice.
- For the educationally challenged students who whine that school is a waste and they can't wait to quit, put a piece of paper and a pencil in front of them and say, "Write down what leads you to believe dropping out of school is a smart thing to do. If it makes sense, I'm on your side."

- In a courtroom, lawyers will argue the law if the law is on their side. They'll argue the truth if the truth is on their side. If they have neither going for them, they'll talk fast and pound the table a lot. Some students are doing just that. It's the great cover-up, perfected by some who know they are going down the wrong road but won't admit it. I call it "living the lie."
- A student's job is to learn as much as possible in order to realize his or her full human potential. Our job as teachers is to help our students do their job better. Period.
- Children who are not required to grow rarely do. Look around your class-room at sixteen- and seventeen-year-olds insisting on acting like second-graders. You get the picture.
- Intelligence is the best line of defense against poverty.
- In our haste to get this thing done, in our haste to rush these kids out the door, diploma in hand, patting ourselves on the back for bringing the project in on time, we continually miss the most vital cog in the wheel. Leaving this cog out will collapse the wheel somewhere down the road. Being an avid but severely challenged golfer, I recall a lesson a teaching professional swore by that made so much sense that I still attempt to adhere to it to this day. It's applicable not only to golf but also to everyday life. The address of the ball, the "setup," is the most important step in a golf swing. If this vital part of the swing is not right, nothing that follows can be right. If these kids had their diplomas "handed" to them instead of us educators insisting they earn them, nothing that follows can be right.

Chapter Fourteen

The Direct Approach

What you want must be what your students want—or very close to it. It must at least be in the same ballpark. If not on the same page, then in the same book. Most students are not mature enough to adapt to your wants. Plus, they don't care what you want—especially your behavior-problem kids! They'll take the opposite side just to tick you off.

Remember these two salient facts:

1. To sell someone something, you must talk in terms of what they want.
2. You are the grownup. You have the ability and the responsibility to be flexible.

You must adapt according to the student you are trying to reach, whether it's to improve their grades or change the course of their behavior. And since we're talking here about the latter, it is imperative to know what their wants are. How do you do that? Take the direct approach. Eliminate the guesswork. Get right to the heart of the matter. Cut to the chase. Ask them, point blank, what they want—with finesse, of course.

A car salesman who knows his business asks a series of questions during his initial contact with a prospective buyer to determine which direction he should take to make the sale. If he is smooth (the finesse), knows his business, and probes in a nonthreatening manner, the buyer will willingly offer this information. After all, the buyer doesn't want to waste time. He didn't stop in to the dealership for a chit chat. He's saying, "This is what I want. What do you have that fits what I'm in the market for?"

A side note: chances are the buyer will stop into a dealership where he knows and trusts the owner and/or the salesman. Remember that. That's you.

I asked my students, this time in an alternative education class, "If you could be anything you wanted to be, and success in this endeavor could be guaranteed, what would you be?" For this group, I added one proviso: try to keep it legal. I told them to write it down on an index card. "It's between you and me."

Everyone turned in an index card with something on it. The responses were surprising and quite revealing. Some were well-thought-out, and some, shall we say, lacked reality. Some students had forgotten about the legal part. But that was okay. It gave me a starting place with each student. I could (and you can, too) work with that to their advantage and my own.

I had asked in a nonthreatening way what they wanted. I took failure out of the equation and put success in as a given. All limits were now gone. I wanted to see where these kids' heads were. What were they thinking and not sharing with anyone else? Did they have a dream? What was their vision for their future? Had they even thought about it? Was it doable or was it pie in the sky? Did they really give a damn about where they were headed?

I took the direct approach. I asked and they answered. Now what was I going to do with it?

~

OBSERVATIONS

- The government requires all drug manufacturers to list the many adverse side effects that can accompany their product. What if schools listed and distributed to every student the adverse effects that can be visited upon them tomorrow for their empty-headed decisions today?
- For you to get students to want to change, you have to convince them that what you're offering is better than what they have.
- "Success is not a destination, it's a journey. I believe the practice and the preparation to get there is the most important thing." —John Wooden, American basketball coach
- Students: What exactly, from past experiences suffered by those who chose to go down the same road you seem intent on going down also, attracts you? Is it the poverty, the odds of ending up confined to a jail cell, or just the general overall hopelessness those other souls have had to endure? Just wondering.
- "Rarely do we find a man who willingly engages in hard, solid thinking. There is almost a universal quest for easy answers and half-baked solutions. Nothing pains some people more than having to think." —Dr. Martin Luther King Jr., activist

- "You cannot exaggerate how often and how simply you have to say things in public life to get this country's attention." —Daniel Patrick Moynihan, U.S. senator

Chapter Fifteen

Picture This

"If you could see what you look like, you wouldn't ever do that again!" Did your mother ever tell you that? Mine did. Visualization is a powerful tool. It brings words to life. It gives them form and shape. It colorizes them. It can transform a relatively bland concept into a dynamic image.

Remember that everyone (including you and your fellow teachers) wishes for something. Now you have the opportunity to put a face on this thing. Why is this so important? Here's a quick demonstration with you as the subject.

Close your eyes. Now conjure up the one seemingly impossible thing that you would *love* to do at this point in your life. If it's a fighter pilot at the controls of an F-16 on a dangerous mission, go there. If it's taking the mound for the seventh game in the World Series with all the kids who made fun of you in school in the stands proclaiming that you and they are good friends, go there! Whatever it is, for the next sixty seconds, you are going to create this image in your head. Go!

Okay, now you've opened your eyes. What did it feel like? Did it feel good? Was it euphoria? Would you like it to come true?

Now imagine someone in authority telling you it is entirely possible. It's doable. And they are going to help you make it—whatever it is—come true. It's going to happen!

Remember, students are driven by two basic things: *they want something to happen or they want something not to happen.* But if what they want seems so far out of the realm of possibility, they lose hope. A kid without hope, a kid who can't see their future, is a bored kid.

A bored kid who can't see an education as a means of achieving anything is a likely candidate for dropping out. Even if they are not old enough to drop out, they are certainly old enough to create problems for you. They are *in-*

school dropouts, treading water and taking up space. And whether you like it or not, you have to deal with them. I'm sure a few names and faces just popped into your head (there's that visualization again).

They're bored and without hope. Learning the new things you're pushing is of little importance because they just don't see what it has to do with anything. (I have heard this from so many students, I've lost count.) How do your classes stack up? Do they have a direct bearing on their lives and their futures that seems plausible to them? And you're stressed and ready to give up. Both have got to change. Kids and teachers are in danger of quitting, dropping out. But visualizing and then experiencing some success can turn the tide.

Case in point: Jason was a kid who had trouble written all over him: a gangly, likeable kid on the verge of giving up on himself. His English class was assigned to copy a poem of at least ten lines on an index card and memorize it. It would be presented to the whole class the following day.

As the rest of the class busied themselves with the task before them, this kid just sat there. I walked over and inquired if he had already memorized his poem. He shook his head no.

"Why not?" I asked.

"Because I'm stupid," he said.

All the kids at his table laughed; others in the class joined in. I even smiled. The only one not laughing was Jason. I realized quickly that this kid was dead serious. He had convinced himself with the help of others, family members maybe, fellow students no doubt, that he was so stupid it wasn't worth trying.

I took his index card (he had at least selected a poem and written it down) and looked it over. He hadn't picked the easiest poem to memorize, but since he wasn't planning to attempt memorizing it, he didn't care. But it *was* doable. Now the hard part: making this kid believe it was worth the effort to try and memorize this thing.

"How about if I show you how to memorize this in about three minutes?" I asked.

"Yeah, right," he said. Now all eyes were on his table.

"Come up to my desk and bring your card," I said, not giving him time to say no. "The rest of you, get back to work."

Jason plodded in front of me like he was on his way to his own execution. Head hung low, arms hanging straight at his side. He definitely needed a shot of confidence, and so did I. I started to doubt myself. Maybe I had bitten off more than I could chew. But I had made a commitment to this kid before the whole class. There was no turning back now.

I sat down and he stood next to me, "Jason, you and I are going to prove something. Do you know what that is?"

"What?"

"That you can be one of the smartest kids in this class."

"I'm not smart," he said.

I let that pass. Then for the next three minutes I showed him a technique I had learned during a memory class I had taken years ago at a local university. It's simple and I still use it.

Task completed, I told him to go sit down and find something constructive to do (one of my favorite lines that gives me a lot of leeway). Eyes followed this kid back to his table. There was a smile on his face. It was driving the other kids nuts.

With about five minutes left in the period, I stood up and asked, "How many have memorized their poems?" A few hands went up. "The rest of you, make sure you have it down by tomorrow for Mrs. Green."

Then I turned to Jason. Crunch time. This was either going to work, or bomb out big time. I could feel the vibrations from the boom already.

"Would you mind bringing your card up here and reciting your poem for the rest of your classmates today?"

Jason froze. I didn't figure on this.

"Come up here and give it a try. Give me your card."

The take-charge approach. Used with the encouraging intonation, it usually produces the desired results.

"Do the best you can," I instructed Jason as he stood to face twenty-five skeptical but intrigued classmates.

He didn't nail it. But he was damn close. A big smile creased his face— whether from the relief of having gotten through it or the pride in accomplishment, I wasn't sure.

I went further. "Do you think, Jason, you could memorize a twenty-line poem with what I showed you?"

"Sure." The class was now absolutely still. Then further. "How about a thirty-line poem?"

"I'm not sure about that." He shook his head.

"But do you think it's possible with what I showed you?"

"Possible? Oh yeah, it's possible," he said.

Still dead silence. Did this "stupid" kid just say it was possible to memorize a thirty-line poem? I could see the rest of Jason's class attempting to grasp what he just said.

With the period over, Jason got up to leave and was quickly surrounded by kids who wouldn't have given him the time of day forty-two minutes earlier. He entered that classroom convinced he was too stupid to learn anything complex and exited the star of the class. His classmates bombarded him with pleas for him to teach them what he had just learned.

He looked at me and smiled. He didn't say a word. I knew he could see himself in a new light. His life had turned the corner. He now had an opportunity to visualize himself doing practically anything in his imagination. He now, I hoped and believed, would never view himself as stupid again.

Far too many kids have this picture of themselves, and it can be devastating. It can follow them around the rest of their lives. They withdraw or become problem students. They can become a burden to you, to society, and especially to themselves.

Listen closely. Visualization is one of the most powerful tools you have when dealing with students. It's especially powerful with kids who have a poor self-image (which includes almost all your behavior-problem students, and I don't care how cool they think they are).

A kid must see himself as successful. He must have a picture in his mind of flying that jet or pitching that crucial World Series game. He must visualize it . . . with your guidance. It must appear doable. And it must be, in their young minds, worth pursuing.

I gave Jason the means to start dreaming about those things that once seemed impossible. He still had time. He was only in seventh grade.

~

OBSERVATIONS

- "Education is not the filling of a pail, but the lighting of a fire." —William Butler Yeats, Irish poet and playwright
- The trick with raising expectations that can't realistically be filled is this: Where do we go if, by some fluke, we get there, and who do we blame when we don't?

Chapter Sixteen

Step to the Back

Take a seat in the back of the room. That's you up there in front of a classroom full of impressionable, eager(?)-to-learn teenagers. How do you think you're doing? Do you like what you see? Would *you* buy what you're selling? Do you look forward to coming to your class? Are you someone you'd want to learn from? Are you someone you'd *like* to learn from?

A teacher once started his class this way: "I'm having a really bad day and I don't want to be here. Mr. Miller is going to take my place. I better not get any bad reports. Got it?" With a pause for effect followed by a fierce scan of the room, he left. That set the tone for that entire period. What if Mr. Chuckles had stayed for the entire day? I can only imagine what would have gone on in that classroom.

No one expects you to be at the top of your game every day (except a few school board members who are always at the top of *their* game). It isn't possible. Let's remember the cardinal rule when it comes to sales (and you *are* in sales!): the seller is just as important, if not more so, than the product being sold. Almost always, the buyer buys into the seller first—her personality, mannerisms, humor, and the way she presents herself. It's the way she smiles and engages her customer, as well as the way she looks. And, of course, her professionalism and knowledge.

The skilled seller knows that in the first sixty seconds (that Golden Minute) the buyer will decide whether this is someone to do business with. The buyer *must* buy into the seller before he can buy into whatever is being sold. And that is why how you present yourself goes a long way toward how the day goes.

Start a class with a frown, a bark, or a bad mood, and that sets the tone for the rest of the period. Don't be surprised when some of your students return the favor or totally tune you out. It's a defense mechanism. People respond in kind to what you do.

Now, when you're in a good mood and wearing a smile, well, it's catching. You gain a reputation as a good guy and it spreads through the school quickly. Students walk into your classroom already in a good mood. Many times you are their oasis—a welcome change from the mean teacher down the hall. It doesn't matter what subject you teach, they buy into you. Whatever comes next is okay with them. Whatever product (subject) you're pushing seems like a good buy.

One of my teachers, Professor Jones, had the unique ability to put an entire class to sleep as soon as he walked in the room. The man never smiled. He dressed like he was mad at the whole world. He acted as if he thought his subject was the only one on campus. His lectures were bland, delivered in a monotone voice. His classroom was always filled to capacity. How can this be? Attendance was mandatory. Three absences and you failed his course.

The guy didn't really care. He had a captive audience and he would do as he pleased. If that meant boring the heck out of you and treating you like an idiot, so be it.

On the other hand, Professor Smith's classroom was also filled to capacity, but attendance was optional. If you didn't want to go, you didn't have to. But everybody did go. Why? What was the difference between Professor Jones, who would have been great in a "Law and Order" episode as a murder victim who had it coming, and Professor Smith?

Smith knew his subject backward and forward, and so did Jones. But that is where the similarity ended. The enthusiasm Smith brought to the class was contagious. He was funny. He was thoughtful. He was insightful. His storytelling kept the students on the edge of their seats. He used this skill so effectively that he was like a polished actor, delivering his lines with just the right facial expression, tilt of the head, furrowing of the brow, and occasional flick of the hand.

He was quite the entertainer. And while his students were being entertained, they were being educated, often without even knowing it. Now that's smooth. And his students retained what he was saying because of *how it was being presented*. It was positive, uplifting, and enjoyable.

How do you think you're measuring up? You're being judged every day, you know. In every class. By every student. How's your act? Would you pay to see it?

It isn't easy. But with time and practice, you can become a polished entertainer, providing the product of a good education for your students. An education that will stick with them long after they leave the theater.

Are you the yardstick by which students measure every other teacher? If not, why not?

~

OBSERVATIONS

- Some kids are time takers, just trying to burn the clock. They have a willful ignorance.
- A sign fixed to the back cab of an old fire engine read, "There is no hard and fast rule for the operation of ladder, but common sense and good judgment of the operator must be relied upon." The ladder is your classroom. You are the operator.
- Once your students quit buying into you as a decent person, you're finished as an effective leader.
- Being a leader is not about ability; it's about responsibility.
- "I've come to the frightening conclusion that I am the decisive element in the classroom. It's my daily mood that makes the weather. As a teacher, I possess a tremendous power to make a child's life miserable or joyous. I can be a tool of torture or an instrument of inspiration. I can humiliate or humor, hurt or heal. In all situations, it is my response that decides whether a crisis will be escalated or deescalated and a child humanized or dehumanized. I am a part of a team of educators creating a safe, caring and positive learning environment for students and teaching them in a manner that ensures success because all individuals are capable of learning." — Dr. Haim Ginott, Israeli teacher
- You're more than just an educator—you have to be for kids to respond to you with open minds. Look upon yourself as a life-improvement coach.

Chapter Seventeen

Let's Start at the End

Did you ever, just once, sneak a peek at the last chapter of a good novel to see how it ends? Some of you have, and don't deny it. You just can't help it. If the last chapter is a blockbuster and makes you go "Wow" even though you don't know what's going on, you can't wait to read the rest.

Imagine—there's that visualization again—walking into a room, TV blaring, and you just catch the tail end of show of murder and intrigue. It gets your attention. It fascinates you. It mesmerizes you! You ask everyone in the room what it was all about. You *have* to know.

Years ago in a university course, the instructor told us if pressed for time when reading an article, scan the title, all subtitles, and the first two and last two paragraphs. If we did that, we could probably carry on an intelligent conversation about that article. And it works!

So where's this all going?

Your students need something to shoot for. There must be something they want enough to motivate or energize them. Most of these kids are too young, too immature to read the whole book just to get to the last chapter. But you can read the last chapter *to* them. You can tell them, "At the end of my course, this is where you will be. If you follow my instructions, that's how far down the path you will have come. And this is how it will benefit you in school and in life."

Remember the question that young girl in the beginning of this book asked so eloquently? "Why do we need this bull?" It's a valid question! The beginning of the semester is an excellent time to answer it. Because if it is on her mind, you can pretty much bet it has crossed the minds of every other kid.

Put yourself in their shoes. (You've already been there, in case you forgot.) You're a student looking at a four-month class that you really don't want to take. But you can't get out of it. "What a total waste of time," you mutter as you plop yourself into a seat and wait for the first class to begin.

The instructor walks in the first night. You're tired. You really don't want to be there. You'd rather be anywhere else! Preferably home in front of the TV, cold one in hand. "Why me?" rattles around in your head.

The first thing Madame Professor says? "Tonight, we are going to start at the end. Tonight's class will be exactly the same one I'll teach four months from now, when we wind things up." Does she have your attention now?

"And I'll begin with the last two sentences of that night."

Are you really awake now?

"Because you have completed my course successfully, your earning power has now increased ten-fold. Congratulations, and enjoy the money."

Everyone *needs* to know where it's all leading. Is it worth their time and effort? Will all the hard work pay off? You want their attention and cooperation. Let them know what's at the end of the rainbow. If it's worth their while, they're yours.

You can even start each class with a Golden Minute, letting them know what you're covering today and how it will benefit them. Snag their attention in that minute, and the next forty-one go down a lot easier.

OBSERVATIONS

- Our lives are defined by opportunities. Even the ones we miss!
- The stick-and-carrot approach to behavior problems almost always leads to disastrous results, simply because the carrot ultimately loses its appeal and a bigger, fresher one is required.
- When are we going to figure out the object of the game is supposed to be not how many kids we shove out the door with a diploma, but how many kids proudly walk through that door with a diploma they've actually earned?
- "In order to succeed, your desire for success should be greater than your fear of failure." —Bill Cosby, comedian

Chapter Eighteen

And in This Corner

Mark Twain once said, "I have been through some terrible things in my life, some of which actually happened." Faculty rooms are supposed to be places to go to get some work done, unwind, grab a cup of coffee, or just hang out to shoot the breeze. And most of the time they are exactly that. Hence the name teachers' *lounge*. They're an escape, a time to catch your breath and kick back.

But then again, the stress level in that room is sometimes unbearable. The griping about this student or that student—with heads all bobbing in agreement—gets to be too much.

"There's not enough time in a day to do all this stuff!" is also an oft-heard complaint. So after forty-two minutes of slurping java and working yourself up into a lather, you, the overworked public servant, hurry to your next class to do another forty-two minutes of battle. As one teacher put it aptly, "Back to the war." If you wake up every school day with thoughts of *enduring* three or four periods (luckily there are often a few periods of pure joy), you're going to wear out quickly.

Ask yourself this question: What is the difference between those joyous classes and the ones you absolutely dread? Sure, the students are different. All the maniacs seem to end up in the same class, right? (How *does* that happen?) But the room is the same; the air is the same. The lighting is the same; the material is the same. The one thing that's different, besides the students, is YOU!

Go to the back of the class again. Take a seat. Now focus on the teacher (that's you) standing in front. What do you see? The first you, with the joyous AP class, is relaxed, focused, and stress free. You're at the top of your game. Teaching is fun—as it should be. The other you? You're standing in the hallway waiting for the World Wrestling Federation ring announcer to warble, "Let's get ready to rumble!" You *know* what awaits you every day at this time.

If you could see your mannerisms, your demeanor, your attitude *before* those two classes, you would say, "That's two different people!" And right you are. It's like Dr. Jekyll and Mr. Hyde. And don't think for even a second that your students don't know it. Attitudes work both ways. Attitudes are contagious. Attitudes can set the tone for a business meeting, a presidential news conference, or a pregame rally. And yes, oh yes, your attitude can set the tone for the way your classes go that day.

Harken back to your college days. Some professors seemed to be in a good mood always. Others could have starred with Matthau and Lemmon in *Grumpy Old Men*. Whose class did you like most? In whose classes were you most relaxed? Whose class did you look forward to? Which professor did you want to be like when it was your chance to stand before a classroom full of eager students?

Yet at times, we all morph into Mr. Hyde without realizing it. How can you tell when this process is about to take over your body and mind? There's a reluctance to leave the confines of the teacher's lounge, a tightening of the face muscles, a slowing of your gait as you make your way down the hall chewing several Rolaids. As you approach the mat (classroom), ready to vault over the ropes and into the fight, the morphing is complete. You have become "Kid Teacher," the baddest person on the planet. Or at least in the school. What the heck happened?

Here's what happened: Your other human side kicked in, the side that goes into defense mode. It takes over in all of us when we *anticipate* problems. We brace. We fortify. We ready ourselves as best we can in order to survive.

How many times have you gone into this mode only to find it wasn't necessary? You feel slightly embarrassed. You hope nobody saw your clenched fist and your readiness to leap at the least provocation.

Sometimes it's too late. The stage has been set. Your opponent (whoever that may be) has picked up the bad vibes and goes into a ready-to-pounce mode, too. We say, in effect, when we vault over the ropes and into the ring, "Don't mess with me. This is my classroom, and I swear, if you cause any problems, heads will roll!"

Your Golden Minute, when you are supposed to be setting up how the period will go, has been sabotaged by, of all people, you! If you see yourself in this scenario, it's time to correct it, because if you don't, you will become your own worst enemy. A scowl will be met with a scowl. A clenched fist will get you a clenched fist.

Why not shock your behavior-challenged class instead? Rather than jumping over the ropes, ready to rumble, which, by the way, they fully expect from you, do something completely out of character. Allow the good twin to take over.

Case in point: The class I was covering was infamous for poor behavior. If you look up *ill-disciplined* in the dictionary, you won't find a definition; you'll find their picture. Time for a little experiment.

The class was in its usual "anything but what we're *supposed* to be doing" mode. So I got their attention and let the good twin take over.

"You obviously have a lot of important things to talk about amongst yourselves. So here's the deal. For the next three minutes, the class is yours. Talk to each other about anything you want. No one will get written up. I promise. At the end of three minutes, the class is mine. I'll expect your undivided attention. Anyone have a problem with that? Speak up now. I need to know."

The class went dead silent, trying to absorb what they just heard. They were going to be allowed to talk freely about anything without repercussions? I could see them trying to wrap their heads around this. Mrs. Smith would never allow this. She would be on top of them the whole class, making their young lives miserable, according to them. I knew her reputation, and they probably were right.

But what Mrs. Smith hadn't figured out was that she was making her own life miserable. She hated this class, and they hated her for hating it. I plopped myself on top of the desk, legs dangling over the side, seemingly not a care in the world and said, "You have until the big hand's on the nine. Go."

Dead silence. Was this a trap? What was I up to? I resisted the urge to say anything else. I just looked around the room, then at the wall clock, then back at the class, praying that the principal didn't walk in. Still no movement. Then some kids started talking to one another, and then a few more joined in, taking advantage of this windfall. When a student looked at me, I just smiled back and looked at the clock.

Before three minutes were up, the class was silent again. It was just as I thought. They really had nothing of importance to say to one another. They were just flapping their gums because it had become the norm. And it pissed off Mrs. Smith so much that it became great sport.

"Is everyone finished talking? You have more than a minute left." Nothing. "Okay, the rest of the period is mine."

I'm sure if Mrs. Smith walked in at that moment, she would have been shocked. She might have stepped back out to check the room number. I had lived up to my end of the bargain. And *every* student lived up to theirs. It cost about five minutes of class time, but the end result was a net gain. A win-win.

And if it didn't work? So what! I could have tried something else. I could have played the heavy at any time! Remember what Mark Twain said—it's all about attitude. You give an incentive to change behavior and you'll find that attitudes change as well.

OBSERVATIONS

- Some kids are hard to deal with because they're not likeable. Some teachers are hard to deal with because they're not likeable.
- "Good teaching is one-quarter preparation and three-quarters pure theater." —Gail Goodwin
- You earn respect not by how you dress, but by how you act.

Chapter Nineteen

You're Going to *What*?

Want to learn something about someone? Open your ears and close your mouth. This sounds like common sense, because it *is* common sense. Yet so many of us (me being among the culprits) violate this simple rule on a regular basis.

When you are in a conversation with someone, and it's the other person's turn to speak, stop and listen! If you agree with them, nod your head in agreement. If the other person is offering food for thought, don't say anything, just ponder. Then ask a probing question such as, "How does that work exactly?" or make a comment such as, "I never thought about that!"

Chances are good—no, great—that the person you are having a conversation with will walk away thinking more highly of you.

The art of simply listening to the other guy has somehow been lost in our hurry to get from here to there. The dividends of being a good listener when a problem student (or any student for that matter) needs to vent can go a long way toward solving that age-old riddle, "What's this kid's problem?"

Does listening to a student's side of things solve anything? Maybe. Maybe not. But it would not make matters worse.

Nobody is asking you to back down. Any sign that can be interpreted as weakness can be quickly exploited. But there is a big difference between backing down and finding a workable solution to behavior problems.

If sitting down with a student and hearing her out makes you uncomfortable, then come up with something better. But don't let this conflict have a negative effect on your class every day. It's counterproductive. A festering wound never heals. It's time to be the adult here. It's time to take charge without backing down.

How would one start such a conversation?

Wrong way: "Morgan, sit down and listen to me. This is my classroom and you're disrupting it. What's your problem anyway?"

Better way: "Morgan, let's talk. You and I have been on the outs all year, and it's partly my fault. I'd like to apologize if I've done something to offend you. Would you mind telling me what that is so I can correct it?"

Then shut up and listen.

Someone once said of Gerry Faust, former Notre Dame football coach, "When you talk with him, he makes you feel like you are the most important person in the world." Wise counsel.

~

OBSERVATIONS

- Given what some of these kids experience on a daily basis in their "home lives," you can certainly understand why they do the things they do. But that doesn't make it smart, and it doesn't mean you have to tolerate it.
- Tolerance can be a great thing. But at what point does it become harmful? Kids need boundaries set by someone whom they look up to. And yet, people of good intention unknowingly inflict damage on a student when they continually put up with poor behavior because they're "aware" of his or her circumstances. You are not doing these kids any good by putting up with their defiance!
- Do you realize how many problems are made worse when left to fester because no one took the time to listen? The next time a student behaves poorly, remember that.

Chapter Twenty

What You're Up Against

On a long stretch of windy country road, a city slicker miscalculated his speed and wound up in a ditch, his car hopelessly stuck. With no cell phone, he was at a loss what to do. Then along came a farmer with a splendid team of horses.

"Do you suppose you could hook your team of horses to my car and pull me out?" he asked. The farmer surveyed the situation, unhooked the horses, and led them down into the ditch. But they balked, and the farmer gave up.

"My horses know best and see this as an impossible task. You need a tow truck," said the farmer, and he went on his way.

A short time later, another farmer came along in an old buggy pulled by an old mule. The city slicker didn't even bother to ask for help. But the old farmer stopped, looked the situation over, and said, "Would you like my mule here to drag your car back up to the road?"

"Thanks. But it's not possible. I need a tow truck."

"Mind if we try anyway?" the farmer asked.

"Be my guest."

In short order, the mule dragged the car back up to the dirt road. The city slicker was amazed. "How did that old mule of yours do it?"

"My mule is blind," the farmer said. "He couldn't see that the task was impossible."

Impossible things are accomplished by people who don't believe in impossibility. Teachers have chosen a job that is as close to impossible as it comes at times. Take a look at what you're up against. Try these just for a start: disrespectful students, disrespectful parents, ungrateful students, ungrateful parents, students who have never matured, parents who have never matured, students who don't have a clue but think they know everything, ditto for parents who have passed these traits on to their children.

You are up against parents who don't understand why you don't relish the privilege of raising—I mean, educating—their children. Parents who don't see any problem allowing their children to run around all hours of the night, then blame *you* for "letting" Junior sleep in class. Parents who have abdicated responsibility to be the authority figure in their child's life, treating school like a babysitting service or detention center. Parents who think Cs and Ds are okay—they wish they had been that smart when they were in school!

Largely due to budget cuts and furloughs, there are administrators who are forced to cram large numbers of students into your classes, then feel obligated to call you on the carpet because Mr. and Mrs. Jones are irate that you flunked their son or daughter. And according to their kid, it's the result of you failing to spend enough time helping them.

There's an ungrateful public convinced you're ripping them off working six hours a day for thirty-six weeks, who don't understand why you need a raise now and then, who resent your college education.

How about a school board—most who haven't been in a classroom in years—passing rules and regulations (mandates) developed by politicians who have no clue what's going on in the classroom. Teachers in third-world countries get far more respect and support than you do. Add another ten reasons of your own.

Is it any wonder that 50 percent of teachers leave the profession within five years?

But there is hope. Make no mistake about it; the things that conspire to keep you from doing your job successfully would immobilize even your toughest critics. Remember, silly people never seem to run out of silly things to say. And there *are* people—parents, students, administrators, and, yes, even politicians—who actually appreciate the job you're doing.

A former student home from college saw me working out at the gym. He came over, shook my hand, and shared some of his experiences at his university. Then he asked, "Are you still teaching in the alternative education program at my high school at night?"

"Yeah," I replied. "Someone has to do it. A lot of these kids would be lost otherwise."

He blew me away when he said, "God bless you for doing that!"

A lot of people feel that way about you. When things get rough, when the waters get choppy, never forget that.

OBSERVATIONS

- It never ceases to amaze me how many townsfolk demand that schools produce a more educated, self-reliant student, when we have them 15 percent of the time and they have them the other 85 percent.
- Excessive meddling in areas we know nothing about almost always makes matters worse. Why is this concept so foreign to those in the seats of power in your state and DC? Why is this not completely understandable? It increases costs, wastes money, and ties the hands of those who are on the front lines in this education thing.
- If you didn't know how to play a game (pick one), would you think it right or even desirable that you got to make up the rules? Theory would take precedence over logic and hands-on experience. People who don't have to walk the halls or stand in front of a classroom full of teenagers, or any student of any age, shouldn't be on the rules committee.
- Nobody would expect a plumber to unclog twenty-five drains all at once or a mechanic to fine-tune twenty-five cars at a time or a neurosurgeon to remove twenty-five tumors from twenty-five different patients before they discard their scrubs. Teachers educate twenty-five kids who have varying degrees of intelligence and drive, some coming from good homes and some coming from not-so-good homes, daily, class after class. Unequalled in any other profession.
- Why do some people who know precious little about what goes on in schools assume that teachers have this ability to make students learn? Would they blame the piano teacher if little Johnny refused to put his fingers on the keys, crying every time mom/dad dragged him kicking and screaming to his next lesson? Nobody can force information into someone else's head if that person (student) refuses to absorb it! The question that needs answering is: Why are they refusing?
- Any parents who think their children will be ready to hit the ground running when they reach the magical age of eighteen, as if this automatically prepares them for the real world and how to deal with real-life situations, are delusional.
- One of the things that drives me nuts is when educators see something that obviously is not working and they want to do more of it.

- We give teachers no means to effectively deal with disruptive behavior when we tie their hands behind their backs and then assail them for not knowing how to manage their classrooms, and then blame them for poor test scores that are adversely affected by students who don't care about the results. It's got to stop!
- When parents have lost some control of their kids, they need to quit looking to teachers and schools to pick up the slack. We're educators. We expect you to do your job and have taught your children, at the very least, to have the discipline and manners to be around other kids and adults. We expect you to have them ready for education, and them to want to be educated, during the few hours we have them. Is that really too much to ask?
- When I watch TV programs that show charter schools holding lotteries for admission, and watch the joy in the eyes of parents who have "won," and the agony in the expressions of those who were not chosen, I just shake my head. Do these schools really have better teachers, or do they have more caring, involved parents and students more eager to learn? Am I the only one who sees this? Somebody has to have the guts to say it, and I just did.
- "Some school districts, not students, suffer from chronic learning disabilities." —Ralph Peters, columnist
- How did we ever get to the point in our society where whoever doesn't get the most blame wins?

Chapter Twenty-One

Turn Down the Volume

Being loud doesn't make you right. It just makes you loud. Do you know how often I've heard students say, "All she does is yell all period"? (Remember, they confide in the sub, especially one they've had before.)

Yelling says one thing to a student, loud and clear (no pun intended): "I want your attention and this is the only way I know how to get it." When teachers raise their voices, it is a clear indication that they've lost control, and that's a dangerous thing with a classroom full of kids.

Everyone within the confines of the four classroom walls needs to know that one person, and one person only, is in charge. When a teacher goes ballistic on a kid, the whole class gets hit by the spray. Your intended target may full well have it coming, but some damage has been done to the whole class, including you. How much damage? That depends on how often you go ballistic. The initial hit, when the class is stunned by the explosion, may give you a false sense that this is the way to go.

Some teachers latch on to the crowd-control method, but the effect is exactly the opposite. It has nothing to do with control, but a total lack of it. It's usually an overreaction to some perceived slight. You've been disrespected in your own classroom. It's all very territorial. It's a wonder some teachers don't mark the four corners of their room with whatever one would use for such tasks.

Your outburst has caused the students who were against you to be further solidified; you just hopped all over one of their own. The students who saw you in a favorable light up to this point now see you in a different light. They're stunned.

So what *does* one do when one has the irresistible impulse to throttle someone? The ability to maintain one's cool under pressure is a learned art that will pay dividends big time. If you can remember this, you can master that art and everything else will fall into place: *lose your cool, and you lose.*

Say the following out loud: "There is only one person in this room that I have absolute control over—me. I'm the one who determines how I'll respond, not them."

Case in point: Two boys, having one of their nitwit moments, just wouldn't shut up even though class was ready to begin. They were openly defiant as they continued to gab away while the rest of the class and I waited. Time for action.

"You guys must have something really important to talk about. Let me know when I can start class," I said, thinking this would do it. It usually did. With all eyes on them, they were getting the attention they set out to get.

But this time that was not enough. They continued to talk to each another, ignoring me. My approach had worked before, but this time it seemed to just embolden them! I walked over to them, all eyes on me now, and said, "If it's that important, take it out in the hall and talk all you want." Dead silence. The boys looked at each other, trying to figure out my angle. Then one asked, "You going to write us up?"

"No."

"What happens if Mrs. Prince (the principal) sees us?" Were they being set up?

"I haven't seen her on the second floor in a long time. But just in case she walks by, take a book with you."

"And you're not going to write us up?"

"No, but you *will* miss an important class. You sure you want to do this?"

"Yeah!" and out the door they went, like two little kids who had just stuck their hand in the cookie jar and gotten away with it. They plopped themselves down on the floor in the hallway, backs against the wall, and continued their discussion, relishing their good fortune. I closed the door.

When the bell rang, the class filed out and the two conversationalists came back into the room to get their books.

"You guys have a good talk?"

"Yeah."

"You know what you missed during class?"

"What?"

"We reviewed for that big test you're having tomorrow. We went over all the answers."

Their dumbfounded expressions told me a life lesson might have been learned. I had remained cool. I hadn't raised my voice. I had left myself the option of trying something else. And when we started the review for the test, most of the kids appreciated it. They were glad they hadn't asked to join tweedle dumb and tweedle dumber.

Case in point: Middle school kids can be a handful for any teacher. Put them in a noisy gym, adrenaline flowing, and problems can quickly escalate. This particular day was not going well for me. I thought every class that came into the gym was deliberately conspiring to drive me nuts. I had had it. I'm sure you all know what I'm talking about.

One class put me over the top and I let loose. I read them the riot act, my voice loud and intimidating. They really had it coming. But one girl continued to ignore me. How dare she! I directed my glare in her direction. She continued to ignore me. I couldn't believe it! Another girl sitting on the gym floor next to her tapped her on the shoulder and pointed in my direction. She finally looked my way and I finished my barrage. God, it felt good. These kids needed some discipline, and I was just the guy for the job. Continuing to glare at her, I finished. There was dead silence.

Then the little girl sitting next to the inattentive student said, "Mr. Miller?"

"What?!"

"She's deaf."

That was the last time I lost my cool and raised my voice in anger for no good reason. And *there is never a good reason.* Sometimes lessons must be learned the hard way.

OBSERVATIONS

- You're going to like some kids better than other kids. It's okay. Don't let anyone tell you differently. It's as natural as liking some members of your family better than others. All kids, no matter what age, have likeable qualities. Find them—for both your sakes.
- School years are the only time students get yelled at for acting their age. Don't get bent all out of shape by kids doing what kids do. It's an extreme reaction to an eight-year-old being an eight-year-old.
- Depression can be silent and easily disguised. Some of these kids are depressed and beaten down. Mental disease is one of the only things you can be diagnosed with and get yelled at for having. Why is that?
- Remain calm but still in charge. It's been described as "calm assertiveness." If you bring tension and emotion to a scene that already has both, bad things are going to happen.
- You are never talking to just one student. You are always talking to the entire class. Before you lose it, take a deep breath and remember this: it may feel good to bring down the hammer on a kid who is completely disruptive and disrespectful to you and the other students. But like a drive-

by shooting, the spray hits everyone. How it affects them, I don't know.
And neither do you.

Chapter Twenty-Two

The Uncompeteable

In the classic movie *The Sting*, starring Paul Newman and Robert Redford, a con man on their team poses as a FBI agent hot on their trail. His mission is to scare off a real detective who's been hounding Redford for passing funny money and stands a good chance of screwing up their next sting.

The first thing the imposter agent says to the real cop in an effort to intimidate and establish superiority is, "Sit down and shut up! Try not to live up to all my expectations!"

How many of us take that same approach when we are trying to control an unruly class? We flex our muscles, stick out our chests, and dare anyone to cross us. "No way! Not in my room! If you've been a problem before *or* for one of my fellow teachers, I've had my sights on you since you came down the hall."

All students, whether AP kids or those with chronic behavior problems, bring something into your classroom from the outside—from the period before, the night before, first thing that morning, or something yet to happen— just weighing on their minds. We do, too. But we're older and more disciplined. We are better able to block it out and get on with the task at hand. We can deal with it later—maybe during our prep period, after school, or when we get home.

They, on the other hand, being young and inexperienced, have a difficult time shoving whatever's on their minds to the side and concentrating solely on your class. You are trying to compete with the uncompeteable (it's not in the dictionary). And you are not going to succeed no matter how far you pump out your chest, flex those biceps, and demand undivided attention. Heck, they don't even give their undivided attention to things they truly *enjoy* for any length of time.

If you sense that something is going on with a class of students who just entered your room, be flexible. You have competition. Take a detour from the planned lesson and find out what that competition is, because it's not going to go away on its own. Deal with it up front on your terms, get it out of the way, and move on. When a whole class can get whatever is causing the buzz out in the open, hash it over, and put it away, you'll find you have gained time, not lost time.

A less distracted student is a far-more attentive student. A more attentive student is a better-behaved student. A better-behaved student is a better learner. Plus, you come across looking like a good guy, which is vital if you want to turn behavior around.

Case in point: High school sophomores are tweeners. They're between— not fully free of the giggles and hormonal fluxes of freshmen, but in sight of young adulthood, though not quite sure how to deal with it. And truth be told, they are slightly afraid of it. They think they are all grown up and love to act the part, but deep down they know it's mostly just that—an act, the state of tween-ness. They resent you for treating them like lowly freshmen (how dare you!), and demand that you treat them like the upperclassmen they've become. This metamorphous takes place over a few short summer months, and by damn, you'd better notice!

These three-months-removed-from-ninth-grade sophomores were so busy chatting and laughing about something that they completely ignored me as I stood before them. A lot of teachers would show absolute authority, yell at them to get their attention, and then pounce. And pounce. And pounce. Until they squash the opposition.

But that is not exactly the best way to fill that Golden Minute.

"Okay, what's up?" I asked after I got their attention.

"Oh, nothing," came an answer, accompanied by giggles, a sure sign that this was some good stuff.

"Look, we're not going on until you tell me. I could use a good laugh! What is it?"

So they told me, the whole class laughing as one of the boys, a real actor, embellished the tale for effect. I laughed along because it *was* funny. And then we proceeded with the lesson, having devoted maybe two minutes to letting them get this out of their system. A net gain, in this case, of forty minutes. If I had jumped all over them at the beginning of class, well, you fill in the rest.

You must accept one undeniable fact: you are not going to beat competition like this. So quit trying. It isn't going to happen. The best you can possibly hope for is to amicably coexist with it. What do I mean by that? I mean this: what is competing for your students' attention is a heck of a lot more appealing than what you are offering. Until you accept that and work around it, your days will be long indeed. Sorry, but that is just the way it is.

Algebra can't compete with the juicy gossip circulating through the school about whatever or whoever. Latin doesn't stand a chance against whatever happened in the parking lot before school. Kids will bring their distractions into the room to share with everyone else. It's called being young. We were all there once. Yet some teachers are so insistent that all forty-two minutes are theirs that they spend the whole period trying to compete with the uncompeteable.

Look at it this way, if *you* have something on your mind that just won't go away, can you concentrate on something else and give it your full attention? No you can't. It's not possible. In *Gone with the Wind* Scarlet O'Hara cries, "If I don't tell someone, I swear, I'll just bust!"

It is rare indeed for any class to come in and sit down, ready and eager to start class when the bell rings. When they don't, you have two options: you can bark them to attention and compete all class long with whatever is causing the buzz, *or* you can find out what the buzz is all about and deal with it up front. Chances are it is something innocuous that only a kid would find interesting. In some instances, it is something that requires your immediate attention. But either way, it is not going away.

Case in point: A rather large eighth-grade class was busily and quietly doing their assignment when halfway through the period something outside caught the attention of those seated near the window. Of course, the rest of the class started looking out the window, too. I could have said, "Okay, you guys haven't completed your assignment. Back to work." But it was obvious to me that it was one of those uncompeteable moments. Whatever was going on outside, whether they knew what is was or not, was far more interesting than what they were doing inside.

"What are you guys looking at?"

"Nothing." (The response all kids give when they think they're in trouble.)

"Something's got your attention. I'd just like to know what. Nobody is in trouble."

"A helicopter just went down behind those trees!"

One boy pointed out the window. Now the other kids who didn't know what they were looking for were definitely interested.

"Okay, everybody over to the window and have a better look," I directed.

Twenty-five eighth graders scrambled to get a better look, standing shoulder to shoulder, gazing out the window at nothing. One minute later, they all drifted back to their seats with my assurance that if anything exciting happened with the downed helicopter, I would immediately alert them so they could make a return trip to the window.

All in all, we expended two minutes on the phantom helicopter and I had my class back on task once again, fully engaged, their curiosity satisfied.

What you can't compete with, you can only hope to coexist with. It usually takes very little time out of the period. It saves you from constantly having to stay on top of them. And it shows you are a completely reasonable human being in their estimation.

The uncompeteable. Learn to live with it, or it will eat you up.

OBSERVATION

- Why are cell phones and texting considered a distraction when driving but cell phones and iPods in school aren't?

Chapter Twenty-Three

Why Me?

For constructive change to take place between you and a problem student, someone must initiate the process. It must be someone you trust and can count on to do the right thing. Above all, it must be someone who has you *and* your student's best interests at heart. Can you think of a better person for the job than you?

President Harry Truman, when asked to define what a leader is, said, "A leader is someone who can get someone else to do something they really don't want to do, and like it."

It's your classroom. You're the leader. It is your responsibility to set the example for how the period is going to play out. And believe it or not, your students fully expect you to live up to this responsibility. Even your behavior-problem students!

You and you alone set the parameters for acceptable behavior. They must be clear and concise. There can be no misinterpretations. There can be no loopholes. What is acceptable should be made clear from the start, when a new class of students takes their seats for the first time. (Although you can start at any time, it's more effective when you hit the ground running.)

When asked by another delegate of the Continental Congress what purpose a Declaration of Independence would serve, Thomas Jefferson said, "To place before mankind the subject of the matter, in terms so plain and simple, as to command their assent." Some students actually don't know what's expected of them when it comes to behavior. Nobody ever explained it to them in terms so plain and simple that they couldn't screw it up if they tried.

One teacher allows something that another teacher frowns upon. Another teacher allows something once a semester that another teacher allows one day each week. Some teachers allow gum chewing and others have a strict rule against it. One parent allows something with a wink and a nod and another parent forbids it. All this back-and-forth stuff creates confusion in and out of the classroom. For a kid who has trouble controlling his behavior to begin with, it's a recipe for disaster.

You can't control what other teachers allow and you can't control what goes on in a student's home, but you *can* control what goes on in your classroom. You may not be as eloquent as Mr. Jefferson, but you can state your classroom code of conduct in plain-and-simple terms so no student can claim, "I didn't know!"

When rules are unambiguous, reasonable, apply to everyone, and *are enforced*, the majority of students will not only follow them but also actually appreciate knowing where the line is drawn.

Case in point: Coaching a girl's high school tennis team with forty members can be challenging to say the least. Establishing a set of rules that everyone *could* follow and *wanted* to follow was imperative. A set of ten rules was already in place. They were simple, unambiguous, and totally reasonable for the well-being of the whole team. But we went one step further. We put these rules in writing, like a contract. We made two copies for each team member with places for two signatures: the team member's and a parent's or guardian's. The coaches kept one signed copy; the team member and parent kept the other.

The entire season was problem-free. Even when there was a challenge from a player or parent, we had it covered. We did draw parents into the mix, and involving them from the start had much better results than meeting them for the first time during a problem situation.

~

OBSERVATIONS

- The ideal time to begin a student's preparation for the world of reality is not tenth or eleventh or twelfth grade. That's too late! The time to begin learning this, or anything else for that matter, is when all kids are still eager to learn and have an unquenchable thirst for knowledge. That's first, second, and third grade. General Douglas MacArthur said, "All military defeats can be described in two words: Too Late!"

- A former student once told me of an epiphany that changed her life. She said, "I was just sitting there one day and it occurred to me, I'm not stupid! Why am I acting stupid?"

- Some students are so damaged you have to wonder how they got this far. Until we recognize and make a concerted effort to repair that damage, we are, as educators, just spinning our wheels. Why is it so difficult to understand that guiding a kid to self-respect and a positive sense of self-worth trumps all else? It must come first if any meaningful learning is to take place. We must plug the hole before we fill it with water.

- Educators help people understand things. We bring order to chaos.
- Think of your classroom as a common area, owned by the public, which needs to be managed properly for the good of everyone in that room.
- You can set yourself up with one good decision. But one bad decision, poorly timed, can have such a deleterious effect that you may never recover.

Chapter Twenty-Four

Additions and Distractions

It is annoying to sit in a movie theater and have someone talk through the whole show. You can't concentrate. You become irritated. It's equally annoying when students talk through your lesson.

When my class and I visited the Gettysburg National Military Park Visitors Center, we saw their featured Electric Map, a relief model of the battlefield illustrating troop movement and strategy through the lighting of tiny colored bulbs as they followed the detail of the dramatic narrative. After a short introduction by a park guide, we were given one final instruction before the lights of the theater were dimmed: "If your child begins to cause a disturbance, kindly remove your child to the outer lobby until he or she is under control so others may enjoy the Electric Map show in silence. Thank you."

Very wise counsel. No student should ever be allowed to disrupt your class just for the sake of disruption. No teacher should ever have to tolerate such behavior.

Certainly, you can differentiate between teenage nonsense and open defiance. It's a challenge to your authority and a challenge to your standing as an educator. It's an assault on the rest of your students' education as well. It makes a mockery of the rules set in place to support a learning environment.

For some reason, some teachers put up with this type of behavior on a daily basis. They may be intimidated by the student, the administrators, the parents, or a combination of all three. This means the other students are forced to put up with it, too. It's not fair to anyone.

Take a seat in the back of your room again. What do you see? What do you hear? What do you feel? Do you see a struggle to present the lesson while periodically disciplining "the rebel without a cause"? Do you hear your voice going up and down while your emotions do the same? Do you feel slighted? Cheated? Annoyed that this rudeness continues, day after day? You feel bad for you, but worst of all, you feel bad for the other students who are subjected to this anarchy.

Listen closely, because this must be said: *if you cannot eliminate the problem, you must eliminate the student who is causing the problem.* Some kids, for myriad reasons, are not ready to be around other kids in an educational setting. The two major reasons are: (1) a lack of values that should have been instilled during a child's growing years, and (2) a lack of consistency in the school when it comes to discipline. Which means when a student does something wrong, it will be addressed and not ignored. Please keep this in mind: regulations foisted upon schools oftentimes prevent administrators from doing what they know is necessary to ensure a safe environment where success can occur, effectively tying their hands behind their backs.

Have you paid attention to the natural order of status in your chosen profession: teachers to administrators to board members to the real bosses—the parents? You'll notice that you're the low person on the totem pole. The only people lower than you are the students, and that is only temporary, until you make Junior mad, who then complains to his parents. The repercussions cascade down until they hit you on the head, sinking you even lower than the student in question.

Instead of everyone working together to move Junior onward and upward, everybody often has a personal agenda driven by egos so wide they trip up not only themselves but also anyone else who is unfortunate enough to get in the way.

What is the one thing that connects all these different factions (parent, board, administrators, and teachers)? The student. The parents certainly should have a vested interest in the kid. The teachers, board, and administrators certainly want to see that the student succeeds in this world. And when the students are the only ones who don't seem to have any interest in how they do, then you have a behavior problem.

It's incredible how just one child can turn us all against each other. Superintendents point fingers at principals, who point fingers at teachers, who in turn point fingers at parents. How do students get this much power at such a young age? It's handed to them when schools are hobbled by laws and mandates instituted by, in many cases, people who have little experience in the field of education.

And don't dare think even for one moment that the students, especially the ones with behavior problems, don't know they have this power. They do! And they'll play it for all it's worth.

Case in point: Bad things and turmoil invade a school when the troops on the front line (teachers) feel they don't have the respect or backing of the commanding officers (superintendents and principals). Military terms are appropriate here because what I'm about to tell you could be illustrated with something similar to the Electric Map at Gettysburg. In this case, the ingredients for this ongoing battle were not the hostilities of North and South, but the hostile environment created when administrations and teachers were at odds and a volatile situation was left to fester.

Peter, a behavior problem since he arrived on the school scene, found fertile ground to ply his trade when the new principal decided that an open-door policy for students to air their grievances against teachers was the way to go. I can almost hear the chronically disruptive students saying, "Pinch me!"

It did absolutely no good to send a kid who was acting up in class to the principal's office for a course correction. Students could walk in there anytime they wanted and say whatever they wanted—and they knew it. After a few words with Mr. Principal, the student, Peter in this case, would waltz back into class and pick up right where he left off.

One of Peter's teachers was very popular with his students and fellow teachers. He was animated, engaging, and witty, yet extremely frustrated that this kid kept robbing his classmates of their learning time. In fact, all of Peter's teachers had had it. Any attempts to turn this kid around fell on deaf ears.

The last straw was when Peter decided that taking a nap was preferable to doing the class assignment. The teacher took matters into his own hands. (Remember, he knew sending Peter to the office was a waste of time.) He shook the desk to arouse Peter, who, right on cue, fell out of his desk and headed to the office to report some kind of physical abuse. The teacher was immediately suspended without pay. The parents threatened to sue the district if this rotten teacher wasn't fired. He was put on trial for assault, found not guilty, and eventually reinstated as a teacher, but this only after the local papers dragged his good name through the mud.

And Peter? He won again! Now the ground was even more fertile for him and anyone else who craved this type of attention. Wow, talk about hitting the mother lode! Kids were now freer than ever to disrupt every other student's education any time they felt like it.

What's wrong with this picture? This kid had unwittingly stumbled upon and applied a cardinal rule of warfare: when your enemies are at odds (in this case, administrators and teachers), leverage the situation. How does something like this *ever* get this far? Because the adults (supposedly) in charge allow it! When communication breaks down and egos run rampant, do people actually think good things are going to happen? Apparently they did in this school.

What *should* have happened here? Communication between the administrators and teachers needs to be well-established and well-maintained. Otherwise, disruptive students will use the lack thereof to their advantage. The Peters will rule the school.

Perhaps something like this would work: In my fraternity, we had regular meetings called "the Meeting of the Eye." Any member could vent, dress down or up, air a grievance, or offer a solution without repercussion. Wounds were never allowed to fester. Members were subjected to this cleansing and enlightening experience each month, and more often if necessary. It unified members into one cohesive unit. Each brother knew exactly where he stood with the other. Whatever the problem, it had to stop at that meeting.

Keep "the Meeting of the Eye" in mind as you read the next chapter, "The Parent Trap." Instead of fraternity brothers, think teachers, parents, and students. Everyone must work together to find a solution.

Robert Louis Stevenson said, "The cruelest lies are often told in silence." That silence must be broken. Rather than the usual enabling, denying, blaming, and "excusifying," teachers and parents must be up front and honest. As the teacher, lead by your example.

$\sim$

OBSERVATIONS

- If some students are so "dangerous" that police personnel are hired to roam the halls to keep the peace, why are those students permitted to roam the halls in the first place?
- Poor behavior happens in every school where it's allowed to happen.
- I firmly believe that every child should have the privilege of getting a good education. What they shouldn't be able to do is infringe on someone else's privilege to get one.
- Due to a lack of maturity and intellectual development, they have no idea what it takes to make it in the world of reality, let alone just survive. That's our fault. They take chances with their lives, daring to walk across the high wire, not fearing the fall, because we, mom and dad, and every other enabler is right there, holding the safety net tight. Sometimes they must be allowed, for their own good, to hit the sawdust.
- The question should never have been, "If the student who has been removed from class is returned, is it going to bother you, the teacher?" The question should always be, "Is their return going to bother and disrupt the other students' education?" If the answer is yes, they don't come back.
- Sometimes, consequences must be stunning in order to shake loose the "you can't do anything to me" notion some of these students cling to. Kids who disrespect teachers and classmates disrespect themselves.
- Everyone should have the privilege, and the opportunity, to receive a quality education. This privilege was bestowed upon them by the previous generations who fought and died to give them access to it. It's not a right!

It's not an entitlement! I don't believe it was ever meant to be. What they do with this privilege is up to them. What they can't do with this privilege is infringe on any other student's opportunity to that quality education.

- It's been said that genius is knowing when to stop. The one constant in life is its unpredictability. It just seems that it almost never works out like we think it will. Point that out to some of your "teenage geniuses" who think they have "it" all figured out.

Chapter Twenty-Five

The Parent Trap

Wouldn't it be great to be able to phone Mr. or Mrs. Parent and explain what's happening with their little angel in your classroom, good or bad? If you shared good news, they'd love you to death. If you shared not-so-good news—and most of these calls are like this—you would still get their full cooperation. You would tell them what you recommend to get their kid back on track, and they would say, "We're on board. Tell us what needs to be done on our end and consider it done."

Wouldn't it also be great to win the lottery? We both know that you have a better chance of holding the winning ticket than getting a parent's full cooperation—sometimes *any* cooperation—when it comes to their kid.

Understand one salient fact about dealing with many parents: they believe there is a distinct disconnect between your world and theirs. Apples and oranges. It's rare indeed for them to acquiesce to your "superior wisdom" when it comes to what's best for their son or daughter. It's *your* job to teach the three Rs. But *they* have the final say when it comes to raising Junior/Missy because "you work for them" after all.

How often do you hear teachers say after a meeting with parents, "I swear we were talking about two different kids!" To elicit this reaction from parents, teachers often say something like, "I told them what a good boy or girl they had, and in my opinion, with just a little tweaking here and there, he or she would be back on track. Build the kid up, right? That's what I was taught."

Wrong tactic! No wonder the parents didn't know who you were talking about. To get parents to believe the reality of their child in your classroom, you must be *honest* with them. Let them know up front what they need to hear. Once you have "unloaded," assure them that there *is* a workable solution. Everyone will benefit—especially their child, but also *them*. We all have been in meetings (not necessarily parent meetings) where everyone tiptoes around what they are there for, trying a little finesse here, a little psychology there, not wanting to offend anyone or bruise any egos, and nothing ever gets accomplished! It's best to lay it out at the get-go. "This is what we're here for. After careful thought, this is what I think must be done right now. Give me your thoughts."

Then shut up and listen!

Keep in mind the 3 *C*s: you must come across as Competent, Caring, and in Charge! Parents expect all three from you, *especially* the third *C*—in charge. Would you buy into someone who slapped lavish praise on a kid you knew to be a behavior problem? No, you wouldn't. The word *phony* comes to mind. A successful meeting has honesty as its main ingredient. You must state the problem and establish that this behavior cannot and will not be allowed to continue. You must offer a workable solution that benefits everyone involved, *and* offer an action plan for that solution that you and the parents agree on.

Sounds easy, doesn't it? It's a win-win for everyone involved, right? What could possibly go wrong? Almost anything. Be prepared for the following detours parents have been known to throw in your path, as well as their own.

Mike Tyson, former world heavyweight boxing champion, said of an opponent who went on and on about how he was going to crush the champ, "Everybody has a plan, until they get hit." Know this about parents: they will probably be on the defensive before the meeting even gets started. *You* must not be. They may act angry and disappointed in you and your stinking school. Don't be surprised. It's natural for parents to point the finger at someone else. They may take their child's side in this thing. After all, the kid had their ear first and family is family. Don't be shocked.

They may be hostile toward you, as a teacher, and to education in general. Some parents take a dim view of educators telling them what's best for their kid. Don't let it throw you. Allow them to vent. Don't interrupt them with something like, "We need to calm down!" They will eventually run out of steam. Just hang tight. Use this opening salvo to your advantage. Welcome what they're saying and how they are saying it, because it will tell you exactly where they're coming from and who you're dealing with. It will also give you a front-row seat to what your student has to deal with when he or she leaves the building every day.

In short, be prepared for and expect everything they hurl—figuratively, I hope—at you, including the threat of a lawsuit (nothing more than the last refuge of desperate people who have run out of ways to deal with unpleasant situations intelligently). Don't blink. Never let them see you sweat. Keep in mind that all parents believe that their kid is a *reflection on them* for good or bad. There's no way to get around it.

Also, keep in mind that your meeting is not a negotiation. You are not bargaining with them. You are informing them that Junior or Missy is a disruption in your class and that it must end. They make the rules in their house. You make the rules in your classroom. Period.

Now for the easy part: getting them to go along with what you're saying. It's vital that they be on board, on the same page, in the same book. President Lyndon Johnson, when asked how he handled his detractors, said, "I'd rather have them inside the tent pissing out, than outside the tent pissing in."

Whether it's about a suspension from school, expulsion from your class for the remainder of the semester, or something more drastic, it's crucial that parents assume a place *inside* the tent. Parents, like everyone else, do things for one of two reasons: *they want something to happen or they want something not to happen.* They may come into your meeting full of bluster, threats, and ultimatums, finger-pointing all the way. They don't want to be there. All their chest pounding is a cover-up for their *disappointment.* Do you really think they're proud that Junior or Missy is heading down the wrong road? Of course not. They secretly wish their child were a good student and a swell kid to be around.

If they were truthful, they would admit they don't have a clue how to turn this thing around. They're hoping you do, because their child is driving them nuts at home, too. It's just that they don't want to be blamed for it, even though, deep down, they know they need to take some responsibility.

Small messes are easier to clean up than big messes. Talk in terms of what the parents want. Point out what's best for them. Be clear about where their son's or daughter's poor choices are leading them *and leading the parents.* Lay it out in terms "so plain and simple as to command their assent" (Thomas Jefferson). You're not making any of it up. It's not something you concocted to make their lives miserable. You're not on some type of power trip. It's real, it's happening in your classroom, and it's a detriment to the educational process. And it's going to end, here and now!

Nothing is more important to this kid's future than getting this thing resolved and getting him or her back on the right path, now, today, one way or another. You are derelict in your duty to the other students, to your profession, and to society in general if you allow this situation to continue.

The older this kid gets and the longer this destructive behavior is allowed to go unchecked, the harder it's going to be to turn this young life around! Did you know that according to "Elementary School Years: A Replication Study of the Check & Connect Model," by Sandra Christenson, Camilla Lehr, and Mary Sinclair (in the July 2004 issue of *Journal of Education for Students Placed at Risk*), the paths children take in life usually become evident by the third grade?

Read the previous two paragraphs again, slowly. It's imperative you understand that behavior problems are a clear indication that something is wrong. This kid's bad behavior is a byproduct of an underlying problem that's not being dealt with. If not addressed immediately, whatever is wrong is going to get worse. These things don't correct themselves. Chronic poor behavior in school leads to failure, which far too often leads to dropping out.

You, your school, *and* the parents are not doing this student any good by permitting these students to continue down this destructive path. Everybody loses. Everybody! Especially the kid. The long-term negative consequences they'll suffer because no one had the backbone to intervene can, and often does, last a lifetime. That's everybody's lifetime, including their parents'. We're going to help them make an informed choice where to go with this. We're going to point out in a nonjudgmental way that this is not an "us versus them" situation. It has to be "us *with* them," with you taking the lead.

Think in terms of what the parents want and what they don't want. Address their child's future and how it will directly affect *their* future if their kid is allowed to continue to spiral out of control. Tell the parents that there are nights staying up wondering where the wayward offspring is and what they're up to. Late-night phone calls you hesitate to answer because you have a gut feeling that it's not going to be good again. There's the need to answer probing questions from little brothers and sisters about their sibling's whereabouts and why they didn't come home again last night. There's the hoping and praying that "the rebel without a cause" doesn't influence younger siblings to choose a similar destructive path in life.

There are the late-night calls from the police; hitting you up for bail, rent, or food money; needing a place to stay until they "find themselves." There's getting married or living together and needing help because *their* kids need a roof over their heads and food in their bellies. And guess what kind of mate finds your kid special? You get them, too!

Point all this out to them, and while you're at it, point out that there's a good chance that they, working with you and the other teachers, can avoid this train wreck. If everyone works together toward the goal of getting this kid straightened out, maybe one of the above scenarios can be avoided.

Don't let them tell you that school is not important. If they are educated, they know better. If they are not educated, they may resent you because you had the gumption and the means to get a formal education. They probably had lots of opportunities to better themselves, but for reasons known only to them, they chose not to. That's their fault; don't you let them make it yours. There's a good chance the parents giving you the most grief made the same choice their wayward kid is choosing and are now suffering the consequences of that poor choice. They would dearly love to blame someone else.

Our hope is that everyone will work together and do what's right by this kid. If that means dumping him out of your class and making him/her take it over, so be it. If it means tossing her out of school for the remainder of the year, so be it. Whatever it takes, it must be done for the good of this student *and* for the good of the rest of your students.

Need some ammo to back you up?

- 90 percent of high school dropouts are living in poverty by age twenty-six.
- 50 percent of the prison population in the United States is composed of high school dropouts.

If these two facts don't make Mr. and Mrs. Parent sit up, shut up, and listen, call the school nurse to check them for a pulse.

~

OBSERVATIONS

- Time after time parents and guardians who micromanage their children's lives produce youngsters who can't function on their own. Don't they get that?
- What if we gave parents and guardians a bonus check, say $5,000 at the end of each school year, contingent on their seeing to it that their offspring come to school, learn this stuff, be respectful to their teachers, and actually care about education and their own future? Do you suppose they would be a little more diligent?
- If parents are legally responsible for their children's actions, why are they not held accountable when their kids bully and intimidate and rob other kids of their education? Isn't that assault? And shouldn't it be actionable?
- When I hear parents and their belligerent offspring yell, "We have rights!" I wonder if that means the other kids, who are trying to squeeze in an education between disruptions, don't.
- I'd say this to a parent running interference for their son/daughter: My job is to do my best to see that ALL my students have the opportunity to achieve a happy life. Your kid is disrupting my job and their opportunity. And it is going to stop, for the good of all.
- Do we really think the future of the country rests entirely on bringing along, at great expense and dubious results, those students who have chosen to be left behind?
- One of the great faulty assumptions of all time is perpetrated by parents and other adults, and that is this: that somehow we can educate students by keeping them in ignorance for as long as we can about the harsh realities of everyday life. When we protect students, insulating them from these realities, we do everyone a grave disservice.

- Do you suppose parents would be okay with their children going to their workplace every day with disruption as their main goal? Like they do in school?
- When parents keep providing unmotivated, disruptive students with all the creature comforts without requiring anything in return, why should the child bother to change? What's the incentive?
- "Be prepared what you wish for, because you just may get it." Parents and guardians who have made it their mission in life to run interference and "excusify" (my word) for their wayward offspring better be prepared for a lifetime of doing just that.
- The first question parents should ask when told of their child's poor behavior is this: "Should we be concerned?" If it isn't, you're probably in for a rough ride.
- Parents who expect little from their kid are rarely disappointed. Maybe that's their end game all along. When the ball is in their court, they ignore it or have no idea what to do with it. Or they have so much doubt they set a fire as a distraction.
- Most parents are struggling because they have never been down this road before but still insist on digging in their heels. Offer some guidance.
- Some people are so blind they can't see the red flags fluttering in front of them. It's often called denial.
- It's not my intent to come down on parents and guardians. I come down on people who I perceive as part of the problem, not part of the solution. If that happens to be parents, so be it.

Chapter Twenty-Six

A Bucket and a Shot Glass

In a scene from the TV show *Married with Children*, daughter Kelly, an academically challenged student dangerously close to flunking, needs help with her schoolwork. Her father assigns the task to her brother. Several hours later, the brother enters the living room exhausted.

"Well, Bud, how'd you make out?" the father asks.

"Dad, it's like trying to get a bucket full of knowledge into a shot glass."

The daughter isn't the brightest bulb on the marquee and the show's writers love to emphasize that fact. Her dim-wittedness is absolutely hilarious, due, in large part, to the talented actress in the role.

Think of your students as actors trying to learn the part assigned to them. It can be a daunting task. Now imagine them trying to learn six or seven parts of the show (school subjects) all at the same time! We all know the feeling of being overwhelmed by everyday tasks. We, as adults, sometimes just want to throw our hands up and scream, "Enough!" But we take a deep breath and tackle our problems one at a time until they go away, or are at least rendered manageable. Maybe there should be a class devoted to nothing more than teaching students about everyday life and how to deal with its ups and downs, because this is where a lot of your students' behavior problems start.

Behavior-problem students remind me of Howard Beale in the movie *Network*. I half expect them to stand up in the middle of class and scream, "I'm mad as hell, and I'm not going to take it anymore!" If you listen closely, that's what a lot of them *are* saying. Most of their classmates are getting it, so why aren't they?

Try this. Take your worst class, or any class for that matter, and ask them the following question, "If I could show you a way how to get As and Bs with just a little effort on your part, how many of you would be interested?" Almost every hand that's attached to a behavior problem or failing student will shoot up right along with the rest of the class. Why? Why would these kids care what kind of grades they get? Why would they even consider As and Bs worthy of their pursuit, let alone within their grasp?

Here's a better question. Why do some teachers think that these students have no interest in getting better grades? Because these students have convinced themselves that getting good grades is as close to impossible as it gets. And students who fall behind and give up hope are your problem students or dropouts waiting to happen.

So how does a kid who's failing justify it to everyone else? Easy. They convince themselves and anybody else who will listen that it doesn't matter to them. They can do without all this learning! And to demonstrate how little esteem they hold for your class, they disrupt it every chance they get. These students are saying loud and clear, "You may think you're in charge, but not over me! No way. I don't need what you're selling. No one in the class does!"

What do you do with a kid who has lost all hope? Until they can see a brighter future for themselves, until they can see achievement as possible, it *is* like trying to get a bucket full of knowledge into a shot glass. Only this time the shot glass is not a kid who has difficulty learning. It's the kid who has put a lid over that glass and dares you to get anything into it. You try to pry the lid up, but they pull down hard.

You can't *make* anyone learn anything. It's like trying to feed a tight-lipped toddler in a high chair who doesn't want to eat. Does the child know the food is good for her and that you're not being a big meanie? Of course she doesn't. But you keep on fighting the good fight because you know your cause is a noble one.

Do the problem students value and appreciate what you're teaching? Do they know how it will help them in life and realize that it's smart to take the lid off? Most likely, yes. Then why the struggle? Why does this battle go on every day in every school? Just show them who's boss by sending them to in school suspension (ISS) or detention hall, right? Here's a bulletin for you: They couldn't care less! You're just reinforcing who they think they are and emboldening them to take their poor behavior to the next level.

Time and time again I see the same students assigned some form of punishment. Just the sheer number of times this happens is a clear indication not that it's not having any effect but that it's having the *opposite* effect. Do you want to punish or do you want to change behavior? Until you can answer that honestly, you're going to have problems, because the two are incompatible. Some of these kids view the frequent trips to ISS, detention hall, even out-of-school suspension as an honor. The only thing missing is the badge on their chest that reads, "Look at me. I won again!" The thinking has always been that if you punish these kids often enough, you'll break them. Please! Cut yourself a break!

Punishment may work for small children because you take something away from them that they really want—play time, toys, and such. But when we carry this thinking over to our problem-behavior students, we're shocked that it doesn't change behavior. Yes, it gets them out of our hair for a while. But I can hear most of them saying, like Arnold Schwarzenegger, "I'll be back!" What, exactly, are you taking away from them that they really want? Nothing! They're not getting what you're teaching in class. They know full well they appear dumb and are using defiance and indifference as a shield.

We all can differentiate between students who are never going to fully get it (Kelly, in *Married with Children*) from students who *choose* not to get it. Do we really believe by punishing these kids that they will all of a sudden see the light and miraculously change? Or are we playing right into their hands? If you want someone to change, you must give them a reason to want to change, something they not only can believe in, but also *want to believe in*.

And here's the most important part: you must allow them to save face. Nudge them in the right direction and allow them to reinvent themselves on their own terms.

Case in point: Some kids bounce around detention and in and out of school suspension so often you would think it was part of their schedule! English, period 1; social studies, period 2; in-school suspension every Tuesday and Thursday; detention every odd day; and physical education last period in order to give the prisoner some exercise.

Zeke had one of these schedules all through middle school and brought his defiance with him to the high school. I'll admit he was a handful. Belligerent, actually. You said up, he said down. Or he'd just refuse to participate, which suited most of the teachers just fine, as long as he didn't bother anyone else.

Zeke had flunked a course and was taking it over. It wasn't that he couldn't do the work—he was smart and a likeable kid when you got to know him—but the lid was on, and the harder a teacher tried to pry it off, the harder he pulled down.

When I was subbing in Zeke's class, I remembered something I had read in Dale Carnegie's *How to Win Friends and Influence People*: give a person a fine reputation to live up to. So I called Zeke up to my desk one day and said, "I know you know this computer tech stuff. What are you doing back in this class?"

"Mr. Smith flunked me last year. I missed by one lousy point!"

"That's all? He got something against you?" I knew the answer already. "Listen, I need some help here. A lot of these kids aren't getting this assignment. I know you already know it. Would you be my student teacher today? Help some of these kids out?"

Even if Zeke said no, I hadn't lost anything.

"Okay," he said. So I took the fine reputation to the next level.

"Listen up, everyone. Zeke knows how to do this stuff backward and forward. He's agreed to help me out today. If anybody needs some help, raise your hand and Zeke will guide you through your assignment." To my relief, several hands went up.

"You're on, Zeke." And off he went in his new role as student teacher. And he loved it— the attention and the "thanks for the help, Zeke" comments. The other kids called out his name for help so often that I finally had to say, "Listen, be patient. Zeke's only one person. He'll get around to you as quickly as he can."

Mrs. White, his regular teacher, saw me in the faculty room the next day. "Did you say something to Zeke yesterday?"

"Why do you ask?"

"He wanted to know if he could help me out today!"

"And did he?"

"He was great. What did you do?"

"I gave him a fine reputation to live up to, that's all."

This sophomore became one of Mrs. White's best students. I spoke to Zeke just yesterday. More than two months had passed.

"What kind of grade are you getting in Mrs. White's class?"

"I've got a 100," he grinned proudly.

You must nudge them in the right direction. You must allow them to reinvent themselves on their own terms.

OBSERVATIONS

- Who decided that eighteen is the magical age to graduate from high school? This antiquated notion needs to be long gone. Kids develop at different speeds.
- It's kind of useless to keep applying pressure on the lid of boiling pot of water, only to have that lid pop up somewhere else. The only logical thing is to put an end to whatever is causing the water to boil over in the first place.
- Some kids are doing what they're doing just to annoy you. That, by the way, is having influence over you. The question you must ask yourself is: Why are they succeeding?
- There is only one thing all these kids know for sure: how they feel.
- One of the biggest faulty assumptions is every kid needs to be shoved out the door by eighteen years old. Students run at different speeds. Some kids jump higher than other kids. Some kids process information slower (or quicker) than other kids.

- Someone once said the nice thing about tomorrow is it can be the start of a new day or a continuation of the last. It's a choice. When we keep on bailing them out, we are not doing them any good. They are not growing. It is simply a continuation of the previous day.

Chapter Twenty-Seven

You Deserve a Break Today

Why do we allow stress, anger, or any threat to our authority control us? The least little infraction, perceived disrespect, or anything that does not fit into our neatly constructed plans for the day sets us off! Whether we display anger or internalize it, everything from the point that we allow it to control us on is affected. If you have more days like this than not, if even one or two angry days a week are par for you, you may start to seriously rethink your decision to be a teacher.

Pause. Take a deep breath. Don't do anything rash. It doesn't have to be like this. Your school day, any day for that matter, doesn't have to be a train wreck waiting to happen.

You have very little control over how events will unfold throughout the day. However, you *do* have control over how you react to those events. Some of us have made anger a natural part of our day. It takes its accumulated toll on us, doing nasty things to us physically and mentally, following from the classroom to home and back, wreaking havoc on everything it touches.

Give yourself a one-day break from anger and its stress.

First thing upon waking tomorrow, decide that *you are not going to get angry for any reason.* You will not allow anything to get in the way of this peaceful, stress-less day you have gifted yourself. You are going to render irrelevant everything and anything that would normally upset you.

Here's how you can do that: Carry a notepad. Instead of getting angry, jot down what's causing your anger. Then cross it out with a big *X*. Smile to yourself and continue your day. When you wake up the next morning, take a look at your notebook. You'll marvel at the things you wrote down and crossed out. What you listed as things that made you angry will seem trivial, hardly even worth your time to write them down, never mind cross them out. You'll look back with surprise at how smoothly the day went!

What does any of this have to do with teaching? Plenty. If school isn't fun anymore, the reason may lie with the little things that trigger anger. And if school isn't fun for you, I can guarantee that your displeasure is spilling all over your students. Angry teachers produce disgruntled, unhappy students who most often put a voice to their unhappiness by acting out in inappropriate ways. They can't tell you to do something about your disposition, so they behave poorly and *add to* the problem!

Is refusing to get angry or upset, just letting everything roll off your back, easy? No. Especially at first. But trying it for one day is a start. It's also a great way to find out who you really are. And that's important, because a lot of your students, especially your behavior-problem students, are trying to figure that out or have already come to their own conclusions!

Give yourself the day off from anger, from thinking the worst of everyone, from approaching the day like the survival of the planet depends on staying on top of every single student. Life is to be enjoyed. It should be fun. School is to be enjoyed. It should be fun. Quit taking the fun out of it. Remember that old McDonald's ad: "You deserve a break today!"

~

OBSERVATIONS

- Start each day like you're doing it on purpose. Walk like you have some place to go. Stop blaming everyone else for your problems.
- To the teachers who are considering chucking it all because you've had it up to *here* with poor behavior and lack of discipline: Why would you let the very people you are trying to help drive you out?
- School is about as fun or as stressful as you want to make it.
- It's not what you're called; it's what you answer to that defines who you are.
- I once taught the wrong lesson to a class of sixth graders. Respectfully, they sat silently through something that had nothing to do with what they were currently learning. And silly old me? I thought I had completely captivated them! I informed their regular teacher the next day of my error. But on the bright side, I said, I was brilliant! Keep a smile on your face. It will come in handy in this business.
- Teachers: Enjoy yourselves in school. You're going to be there the rest of the day.

Chapter Twenty-Eight

Push, Shove, or Pull . . .

Give me your tired, your poor, your huddled masses, yearning to be . . . educated. And they're all yearning to be educated, right? Maybe not, but no matter who shows up at your classroom door, the responsibility falls upon you to mold, shape, whittle down and build back up, sand, varnish, polish, and, yes, educate every one of them, turning out student after student well prepared for the real world. You're not just an educator; you're a miracle worker!

But that's not how some taxpayers see it. Some say teachers getting paid extraordinary amounts of money to work only seven hours a day—which is probably closer to ten to twelve hours a day if you count creating new lessons and refining old ones, doing after-school tutoring, grading papers, making phone calls to parents, and answering countless emails—thirty-six weeks a year. Teachers had better able to produce kids who can think for themselves, handle basic math, speak the King's English, aspire to higher learning, and become productive members of society! Every single one of them. If teachers worked in the "real world," they say, many would have been fired long ago. Look at students today! Schools are putting out an inferior product!

The most mind-boggling thing I ever read supporting this view was the supposed wisdom of a businessman who allegedly said, "If I kept putting out an inferior product, my company would be out of business. Why do we keep teachers on the job who keep putting out inferior products?" He said if his company was judged by the quality of their finished product, then, by damn, so should schools. Anyone who didn't measure up should be replaced—replaced with a younger, less experienced teacher who would be paid less, too.

Wouldn't you love to ask Mr. Big Business about the quality control at his plant? Is he very particular about the raw materials he uses? If the raw materials don't meet his standards, does he refuse to accept them?

You can see where this is going. Teachers and administrators can't pick and choose the raw material that shows up on the loading dock. We can't reject a shipment because it doesn't meet specifications. We must accept every kid who shows up at the door, no matter how broken the home, no matter how unprepared for the school setting, no matter what the psychological problem, no matter how immature, no matter how ill-disciplined, no matter how disruptive, no matter how rude, no matter whether alcohol or drugs are involved (feel free to add a few of your own "no matters"). Every student comes with their own story—good, bad, or somewhere in between—and we welcome them. Sometimes reluctantly, sometimes with a certain amount of apprehension. But we do take them in and try to mold them into better-adjusted, happier human beings who will one day appreciate the education they received and use it wisely, hopefully for the betterment of all.

In no other business but teaching will you find willingness, even *eagerness*, to take on the daunting challenge of shaping the next generation. From that raw material at the classroom door. No matter what.

∽

OBSERVATIONS

- Failure is necessary for any school system to thrive. No failure leads to complacency. Without failure, we would never know what needs fixing.
- Some people have to be dragged kicking and screaming to a better life.
- Former professional tennis player Brad Gilbert was once asked how he managed to win matches against players who were, quite frankly, better than he was. "I don't try to play up to my opponent's ability; I try to drag them down to mine." Some kids are pros at this dragging-down business.
- Keep an eye out for students who are vulnerable to poor outside influences. That's all of them, by the way.
- The four years in high school are years these students will never get back. But what gets glossed over is the fact that our society doesn't get them back either. The product coming off the assembly line is what we have to live with, as a country, for the next fifty or sixty years.
- Only a handful of people have had the courage to step forward and say, "Bring it on!" That's you. You help shape and mold the next generation of scientists, doctors, carpenters, engineers, professors, plumbers, electricians, and people of the cloth. And you do it for generation after generation. There are good and decent people ready, able, and willing to carry on

without us because of you. You provide our future leaders with the basics necessary to build upon and grow into the citizens this country needs to survive and thrive in this crazy world we live in.

- You inspire kids to dream bigger and look skyward. You give hope to young people when hope is all they have. You are a refreshing oasis for children who have been beaten down by some really crappy beginnings and just want someone to tell them, "Everything is going to be alright. I'm right here." Always hold your head up high. If anyone deserves to strike that pose, it is all of you.

Chapter Twenty-Nine

Outrunning a Tornado

Most kids' perception of the real world is based on things they hear about, read about, see on TV and in the movies, or things they have just conjured up in their own minds. Oftentimes it's based on how they wish the world worked. Rarely is it based on how the world really works. The older students get, the more ingrained these false concepts become. They convince themselves that they have figured out this thing called life and they challenge, even defy anyone—especially parents and teachers—to tell them any different.

Some students eventually realize that their concept of real life is nothing more than wishful thinking and youthful arrogance. But they cannot back down. To do so would mean they were wrong all along. They can't let their peers see them capitulate to superior wisdom. They will defend what they believe (even if they don't truly believe it) with every fiber of their being. They have to be right; you have to be wrong. It is the *only* way, in their humble opinion (which is rarely humble). They've sold themselves on this junk thinking and will do their best to sell the idea to anyone else who will give them an ear. Add in those other ears and, voila, you have a clique of behavior-problem students ready, willing, and able to wreak havoc in your classroom.

The leader now has self-verification, and so does everyone else in this little group. Everyone likes to be looked up to, even if it's for all the wrong reasons. Anything that puts them on top of the heap. To belong to and be accepted in a group that has at its center one of these mythical leaders is every kid's dream. It's especially true for kids who feel rejected, ignored, even shunned by the "in" crowd, as well as those who feel rejected, ignored, or unloved in their own homes.

Regardless of how tough or how cool they think they are, how anti-this and anti-that they've become, there is usually a core reason disruptive students have chosen to become what they've become. It's called survival. We all have this instinct. Without it we'd perish. We wouldn't know when to back away from a potentially dangerous situation. We wouldn't make wise choices regarding our well-being. We would tempt fate when it was a really idiotic thing to do.

Welcome to the world of the chronic-behavior-problem students. They aren't born this way. A series of events has brought them to this point. It's how they've chosen to survive. And with enough practice, a willing audience, and the right atmosphere, they have all the ingredients necessary to disrupt your class.

They have two options for survival: conform to the rest of the class's behavior or start their own group—even if they are the only members of that group. Since they don't fit in with the former, they choose the latter. They need self-verification. If they can't find someone to give it, they'll give it to themselves. If that means acting up now and again or playing the role of class clown to get it, so be it.

If you let it all get to you, and many teachers do—me included—you are giving them exactly what they want. You are saying, in effect, "You are who you think you are, and I am now verifying it for you and everybody else in this class. You've won this round. You've diverted my attention away from the rest of the class and directed it toward you."

You've played right into their hands. They are somebody! The person in charge in the classroom has unwittingly acknowledged that fact to them and every other kid. Be sure of one thing: how this round plays out determines how the next round goes. And there will be a next round!

What does one do when constantly confronted with disruptive, attention-craving behavior?

Let's go back to the first three sentences of this chapter to get an answer. This is where a lot of attention-craving stuff originates in my opinion. *Most kids' concept of the real world is based on things they hear about, read about, see on TV and in the movies, or things they have just conjured up in their own minds. Oftentimes it's based on how they* wish *the world worked. Rarely is it based on how the world really works.*

Attention-getting behavior will change only when students believe it's in their best interest to change. This is where you come in. I once told a student on an attention-getting kick, "I'm starting to believe you really don't know any better." I was right, he didn't. He didn't understand the basic concepts of everyday life. But he thought he did! Every disruption was an attempt by this kid to say to his peers, "Pay attention to me, not the teacher." Until you get this student to at least start to accept the fact that he doesn't know everything and neither do you (just more than he does at the present time), you are going to go round after round in this endless fight for attention.

Your challenge is to be vulnerable and believable at the same time. Students think that teachers think they are better than the students. Sit down with these kids and talk *with* them in a nonjudgmental way, and you'll be surprised how open they can be. And they'll see you in a new light.

How do you get kids to open up? By saying things like, "Look, I'm not saying I'm smarter than you. I'm just saying I've been around a lot longer than you. I'm supposed to know more." How could a student dispute this?

One thing you have in your favor is that it's tiring to be the center of attention all the time, especially when a kid starts to doubt himself. Keep this in mind. Your attention-needing student may want to get off the stage. When you notice it, grab the opportunity. You must *lead* students to the conclusion that you know more when it comes to how the real world works. You must *lead* them to the conclusion that it would be wise to listen to you.

There is no shame in listening and learning from someone who has been around a little (a lot) longer than they, just like there is no shame in you listening and learning from them about things they know more about than you (sports, music, technology, movies). They must believe and buy into the fact that we all can learn from each other.

Case in point: During a discussion about a horrific storm in the Midwest, the conversation turned to what one would do if caught in the middle of this upheaval. Students offered practical suggestions on how to survive. One student wasn't buying it. He had his own thoughts on how to deal with a wave of killer tornadoes. He would just run in the opposite direction. It was a no-brainer, according to him. He scoffed at the suggestions to lie flat in a ditch, crouch in a bathtub, or head to the basement. When I told him that just one of the multiple tornadoes was clocked at 60 mph, he said he would hop in a car and beat it that way.

"What if everybody got the same idea?" I asked.

"So what?"

"You're on Interstate 80, pulling away from this thing, hoping you don't run into another one, when a crash occurs up ahead. Traffic comes to a grinding halt. Everybody is all jammed up. This tornado is bearing down on you. It's a mile wide. What do you do now?"

He thought for a moment, the other kids listening intently.

"I don't know." A little more thought. "I guess you can't outrun a tornado."

"It's usually not a smart thing to try."

"I didn't think about that."

"We all have things we don't know or think about. That's why it's important to stay in school."

OBSERVATIONS

- The state of public schools today is somebody's fault and everybody's responsibility to fix. For countless years, the bar for personal responsibility and standards has been lowered in order to keep students in school, thereby defining success through sheer numbers instead of sustained accomplishment. Whoever started this downhill slide is probably long gone. Whoever is left had better figure this thing out, and quick, for everyone's sake.

- When we create and allow to flourish, with a wink and a nod, a permissive atmosphere for some students, where we're just happy they showed up for school, we've also created an insatiable monster and loosed it on the world. Visit the nearest correctional facility and you'll see what I mean. Low standards produce low standards.

- A student of mine in alternative education took exception to my statement that all the students were here for poor attitudes, poor choices, or a combination of the two. I was just plain wrong, she said. I informed her I was just plain right, because that was precisely why they were all there.

- There is very little training in school that prepares students for life on the street. Columnist Ann Coulter may have said it best: "Reality betrays children constantly."

Chapter Thirty

Thanks for the Memory

Webster's dictionary defines *organize* as "to compose in a desired pattern or structure." It defines *memorize* as "to commit to memory." The Bill Miller Dictionary combines the two into *memorganize*: "to commit to memory in a desired pattern or structure to facilitate instant and long-lasting recall." (I do take liberties, but it is my book after all.) *Memorganizing* is not that difficult because it has only two ingredients: a desire and a system.

As we become more *memorganized*, we become more successful. In a previous chapter I spoke of a seventh grader who experienced firsthand the power of conquering something that seemed close to impossible. In Jason's case, it was a simple poem committed to memory in an organized pattern. Jason's success built his confidence, which led to more success.

Success breeds success. But when students fall behind, when they give up hope that this learning thing is ever going to come easy, when they decide that their time could be better spent doing something more enjoyable and far less stressful, you have a breeding ground for dropouts and poor behavior. One subject after another is thrown their way until they finally throw up their hands and say, "Screw it!" They become disillusioned with school, disillusioned with teachers. They look for excuses to get out of doing things because they are frustrated. They convince themselves that all their efforts are fruitless. How does it get this far? Let me use the following illustration to demonstrate.

Case in point: Brad was gung-ho for football. He loved watching it on TV with his dad. He couldn't wait to go out for the team. His dad took him out in the yard once in a while and tossed him the ball. He dropped it on a regular basis. The ball was big; he was small. His dad reassured him that when the time came to join a team, he'd be bigger and things would come easy for him, because he was, after all, a natural ballplayer. He liked when his dad made him feel good about his abilities. He was going to be a star, just like the pros on TV!

The day finally came for Brad to try out for the team. He was excited and enthusiastic. His moment had arrived! Could stardom be far off, he wondered?

The coach lined up the whole team on the fifty-yard line and tossed a ball to each kid to see what he could do. Brad looked down the line as his teammates took their turn. Most of them caught the ball just fine. Some dropped it. Brad was a natural, his dad had told him. He would catch the ball when it flew in his direction.

When the ball came, he reached out his little arms to snag it, but it bounced off his chest and hit the ground with a thud. He became nervous, which confused him. He had never felt like this before, certainly not when he had dropped the ball playing with his dad. What was different this time? He'd catch it next time, that's for sure. But the next time came and went. Brad kept dropping the ball. The thuds got louder and louder.

"How can this be happening?" the little boy thought. "I'm supposed to be a natural." He felt the eyes of the other kids on him. Was he the only one who kept dropping the ball? Panic set in. He secretly wished that the practice was over. The kids who had been dropping the ball were now catching it. He could hear them snicker when the ball fell at his feet. Football wasn't much fun anymore. Brad did everything he could think of to avoid practice. He began to tell his dad he was heading to the field, but instead went to the mall to play games. He was much better at these games, and the pressure was gone to catch that damn ball!

Eventually the coach called Brad's dad to check up on him. Brad's dad was upset to learn his son had stopped going to practice—and was just as upset to hear that his son was not a "natural" football player.

So why did Brad quit football? Could it be because his dad thought the coach would teach him to catch a football and the coach didn't want to take the time to do that?

We, as teachers, keep throwing footballs and are amazed when the kids who drop them eventually quit trying to catch them. The Brads of our schools deserve better. They deserve to be taught how to catch the football. That's why we're here.

How could the coach hope to be successful with a player like Brad? Rather than teach Brad how to catch, he just kept throwing the football (think "content") at him. We need to teach kids how to catch what we're teaching, then make it their own in an organized, systematic way: catch it with the hands and then bring it into the body. Teach the kids how to *memorganize* their minds so learning becomes easier and more enjoyable. Show them how remembering lessons is doable. Teach them a better way to organize and store all the information we hurl their way each day.

One of the best books I've read about memory is *How to Remember Anything* by Dean Vaughn. Its principles are easily understood and applicable to any subject. Teachers can learn these memory techniques and teach them to a classroom of students with little effort and with great success. Rote memorization is not the goal. This program emphasizes organizing the mind so recall is instant. Information is "filed" in the brain in an orderly fashion. It's much like having a Rolodex with all the needed information sitting on top of the desk. Subjects don't get all jumbled up. And surprise of surprises, students become better students. Hope takes the place of despair and confusion. Poor behavior is replaced with acceptable behavior.

These kids *need* a structured method to retain all the information being tossed in their direction. They need a mind that is organized. They need a reliable method to study for tests. I've never understood why schools don't offer something like this, even require it for both teachers *and* students. It's a win-win.

Students who give up hope become behavior problems in the classroom, dropouts waiting to happen. Students given an easy, workable method to succeed . . . well, you finish the sentence.

~

OBSERVATIONS

- "We are what we repeatedly do. Excellence, then, is not an act, but a habit." —Aristotle
- Some students lose hope because they are hopelessly lost. They see no way out and have convinced themselves things are not going to get any better. School has become frustrating and aggravating, so they choose to drop out. It's the path of least resistance, which we all at one time or another choose. It's the "anything is better than this" syndrome. The problem is they have no idea what constitutes the "anything."
- The reason some kids can't figure out how to get from point A to point B is they have no idea where point A is.
- If we don't begin to realistically deal with the fundamental problems underlying our underachieving educational system, and do it with haste, we'd better start polishing off our chariots, because when the collapse comes, it's going to come quickly.

Chapter Thirty-One

A Failure to Communicate

God, grant me the serenity to accept the things I cannot change, the courage to change the things I can, and the wisdom to know the difference. This is such sound advice; why don't we all follow it more closely? The sun is going to rise in the east and set in the west every day. There's nothing we can do about that. A student who doesn't want to learn can't be made to learn. And there's nothing we can do about that either.

We can inspire, excite, motivate, encourage, transport, arouse, fire up, stir, exhilarate, egg on, prompt, goad, energize, make it easy, make it challenging, make it enjoyable, make it fun, pique their interest, stimulate, work up, inflame, invigorate, make it rewarding, badger, coerce, drag along, push ahead, awaken, show the light, even cause an eye-popping, life-changing epiphany. But the one thing we cannot do is make someone learn something they don't want to learn.

We need to get out of the mindset that students are in school to learn as much as they can, and that their teachers are failures if they don't. It has never been that way, and it will never be that way. No matter how much money legislators throw at it, no matter how many quotas administrators mandate, no matter how many disparaging remarks parents make, nothing is going to change it.

Some students *choose* to fail. It's not that they can't do what is necessary to succeed; it's that they won't! And until they make the *choice* not to fail, we, as teachers, are just spinning our wheels and spending less precious time with the students who know that education is necessary for success.

What do you do with a student who has made this self-destructive choice? Remember, we all do things for two reasons: because *we want something to happen or because we don't want something to happen.* The first reason is preferable. It's positive. It gives you something to shoot for rather than something to run away from. The unmotivated, uninspired student taking up space in your classroom is rarely shooting for anything. Ask them what they want to do with their lives and their likely answer is, "I don't know. Get a job, I guess." That's it. Take it further and ask them what kind of job they will get without a good education, and their response is, "I don't know."

Most of these kids are running away from something. Forget their posturing and "I know everything" attitude. They're on the run from something and they're running in the wrong direction. The defiance and poor behavior is a mask covering something they don't want to happen. When you find out what that something is, you can begin to take them from the "you can't make me learn" stage to the "I want to learn" stage.

Sometimes it's necessary to point out in no uncertain terms that what a student absolutely doesn't want to happen is exactly what *is* going to happen if things don't change. For some, their fears can be the impetus needed to change their behavior and outlook toward school and education. But it must be their idea, not yours. In the movie *Cool Hand Luke*, Paul Newman's jailer, exasperated by his attempts to escape despite his continual failure, says, "What we have here is failure to communicate."

Case in point: Casey was a fifteen-year-old student who had been in alternative education several times. The last infraction that brought him back to our school was punching another student. Of course it wasn't his fault; nothing was ever his fault. He always blamed someone else for his problems. Two police officers escorted him into our school an hour late one evening. If the cops hadn't picked him up, Casey said, he would have been on time.

After encouraging a younger student to break one of our rules, Casey instigated a "work stoppage" with the kid because the rule was dumb to begin with. We suspended each boy for two days. As I waited with him for his mother to pick him up, we had a little talk.

"What did you get tossed for this time?" I asked.

"What do you mean?" I love it when kids play this game. I stared at him.

"Oh, I told Roger it was okay to open his soda while we waited in the cafeteria." "Anything else?" I knew the whole story. I wanted to hear his spin.

"It's a dumb rule!"

"Anything else?"

"He was mad, so he didn't log in. Neither did I."

"Because Roger did something stupid, you decided to do something stupid, too?"

A shrug of the shoulders. Time for a different approach.

"What don't you want to happen?"

"What do you mean?" A fair question this time.

"Are you scared of anything? Is there anything you don't ever want to have happen to you?"

A shrug, then, "I don't want to go to jail."

"And yet everything you're doing is just about guaranteeing that's where you'll end up. Ever think about that?"

"Not really."

"You want to go through life poor?"

"No."

"What I said about jail? Same with poor. You're heading straight for a lifetime of poverty, and you, who thinks he's so smart, are too dumb to see it coming."

He just stared at the floor.

"The very people who are doing their best to keep you out of prison and out of the poorhouse are the very people you've decided to go to war with. Does that make any sense to you? Think about that hard."

Schools need a program to acquaint students with the complexities and realities of the real world. What happens to students who strive to get ahead? What happens to those intent on being left behind? It's time for a frank discussion on how the world works, leaving no room for doubt or confusion. This is often referred to as *resiliency*, now implemented in many schools. It's time for students intent on being disruptive and dropping out to face reality and the consequences of their actions.

Some students do things because they *want something to happen*, some because they *don't want something to happen*. See the appendix for a small capsule taken from "Your Life, Your Call," my program for students in this second group.

～

OBSERVATIONS

- Why can't this sign be put on the front entrance of every school: "Shame on you for your lack of effort, and shame on us for accepting it."
- I'm going to say this one time and one time only. Money has nothing to do with it! Give me a dozen students who have a desire to learn, a drafty old barn for a school, and some well-worn textbooks, and I'll produce twelve students well prepared for higher education and the world. And so would you.
- Post the following on your wall: "Choose to stay in school. No bills, summers off, weekends off, holidays off. Choose to dropout, and all bets are off."
- The option of doing nothing should be unacceptable to all students. Yet some cling to it like a security blanket.

- Some people must learn lessons the hard way or embarrass themselves enough times to finally view change as a positive thing.
- I miss the old days, before the lines got blurred by those on the outside making laws "designed" to level the playing field. It was, once upon a time, rather easy, to the trained eye, to distinguish between those students who were legitimately struggling in school and those who simply refused to put forth the effort.
- So many students I observe today don't have the dedication necessary and the passion required for success that people of the previous generations had. Where did we go wrong? Without these two ingredients, nothing else falls into place.
- About the only thing you can count on is this: the ones who are going to be successful are the ones who prepare. It's time some of these kids experience some of the bitter fruit without us holding their hands.

Chapter Thirty-Two

The Tomorrow Gambit

Tomorrow holds such promise that many of us find it far more appealing than today. Why? Perhaps because there's nothing we *can't* do tomorrow. There always are possibilities for the future. The last two lines of the featured song in the Broadway musical *Annie* sum it up: "Tomorrow, tomorrow, I love ya tomorrow! You're always a day away."

In the show, it's supposed to inspire hope for the orphans that a better day is coming. But one can twist the hope and promise right out of tomorrow. When abused and misused, tomorrow leads to a long downhill slide into procrastination, self-imposed stress, and failure.

Poor behavior in school has often been unwittingly encouraged by teachers who allow the tomorrow strategy. Permit a kid with a harebrained excuse and an incomplete or late assignment with that free pass into tomorrow and just watch the havoc you create for the student and yourself. It may not start right away. It may take time for a student to begin to feel a sense of entitlement. But with the help of other teachers who are also enablers, you grease the skids for these kids to start to fall behind. And when they fall behind, they lose hope. When they lose hope, they lose interest in what you're selling. When that happens, you have fertile ground for misbehavior and an increased potential for some of them to pack it in altogether.

It starts when a kid latches onto tomorrow as if it's some kind of lifeline. Add in one willing accomplice (an enabling teacher or parent) who doesn't see the harm that these debilitating twenty-four hours can inflict. Yes, reprieves are sometimes warranted. It's when it becomes a habit, an exception that students fully expect to be granted, that problems begin.

These problems are likely to carry over into adult life with potentially disastrous results. But let's stick to the here and now. Let's focus on students who cause you and everyone else in your class difficulties. Nine out of ten of these students are probably chronic procrastinators. It's an acquired addiction, like cigarettes. That first one leads to the second one, then the third one, and so on. Tomorrows are a quick fix for today's problems. And students who become dependent on these fixes get hooked, often with the approval of a complacent, I-don't-want-to-look-like-a-bad-guy teacher or parent.

You are not doing a kid any favors by permitting him to fall behind and procrastinate. It can lead to a lifelong addiction to tomorrow. Set the ground rules. If you don't accept late work, tell students you don't and outline the consequences. Tell students you don't tolerate tardiness, and explain the consequences. Then enforce those rules. Don't be an enabler. You are in charge.

Tomorrows are contagious. They get passed around from one problem kid to the next. These guys will line up with one excuse after another as soon as word gets around that you are an easy mark. And be aware that parents often side with their children because they, too, have the bad habit of the tomorrow gambit.

Students who are allowed to use tomorrow as just another act in their repertoire—*with* your permission—eventually come to consider it as an acceptable way to do business, an okay thing. And other kids observing this begin to want the same privilege. Now you have a monster of your own making on your hands!

Tomorrows should only be awarded on special occasions at your discretion. Parents may rail against you for being heartless, but keep in mind that they may have been the ones to give the first okay to put it off until tomorrow.

Stand firm. Stand resolute. Don't buckle. It's your classroom. You're in charge. It's a hard lesson, best learned as early in life as possible. Now is a good time to drive this point home. Not tomorrow.

~

OBSERVATIONS

- Some problem kids will always choose the shortest route, the least-complicated path, the task that requires only a marginal effort to complete. And we in the educational field pat them on the back and say, "Hooray for you." If the only standard we set is low, how are they going to survive in the real world?
- Rules are rules. The 65 mph sign along the highway is not a suggestion. We don't get to pick and choose where or when to apply the law. It's applied all the time or it's useless. It's enforced consistently and fairly or it becomes meaningless.

- One of the densest elements in the known universe is laziness.

Chapter Thirty-Three

The Future Is Now

Why do we continually allow certain students to steal valuable time away from students who want to learn?

All kids are basically good; some have taken a wrong turn for a variety of reasons. Peer pressure, poor or absent parenting, bad neighborhoods, lack of supervision, out-of-control brothers/sisters as role models, an absence of rules or structure, inconsistent enforcement of rules, a lack of a positive male/female influence in their lives—it all leads to lost kids who feel unwanted and adrift in life.

When we look into the background of some of these troublemaking kids, we begin to understand why they behave the way they do—or better-stated, why they misbehave. We begin to understand why they are disruptive, defiant, obnoxious, and disrespectful toward their teachers *and* their fellow students. We understand why they have chosen to be a thorn in the side and an obstacle that everyone must work around to achieve a good learning environment.

There are certain kids you just can't reach—not with logic, not with tales about what their lives are going to be like without a good education. Rather, you must accept the following:

- An education alone doesn't adjust behavior in any significant way.
- You're not doing these kids any favors by putting up with their guff.
- You can talk until you are blue in the face about where their poor choices are leading them, but they still won't or can't see it.

One of the most dangerous combinations students can have is overconfidence coupled with inexperience. They have all the answers and choose not to listen to a thing we say. Why? Because they have all the answers already!

And they've probably acquired these answers by listening to some other kids who have convinced them that *they* have all the answers. How do these kids find each other? Like minds attract! They are under the illusion they understand life or they are too embarrassed to admit they don't.

So what do you do with these kids who are chronic behavior problems? Do you put up with their disrespect and disruptions aimed at derailing everything you're trying to accomplish and just accept it as a part of doing business?

Some schools do. They let these teenage rebels roam the halls and wreak as much havoc in the classrooms as they please. A suspension here, a slap on the wrist there, and, like a bad dream, they're back again roaming the hallways and plying their trade, refreshed from a three-day suspension intended to punish them and change their behavior. Here's a bulletin: It isn't punishment, and it isn't changing behavior. It's a mini-vacation rewarded for poor behavior! And when these temporarily incorrigible students need another vacation, they know what it takes to get it.

Most kids are too young to see what the future holds or how they fit it. They are incapable of understanding what their poor choices will inflict on their future *and* the futures of everyone with whom they come in contact.

Listen closely. *Just because they don't get it and have no interest in getting it, it doesn't give them a license to wreak havoc without consequence.* Some students (backed by their parents or guardians) think that the school belongs to them, and they can do in it whatever they please. *This has to stop!* How did things get so out of control? Who's responsible for this mess? We've heard of "Take Back the Night," the international movement demanding the right of women to move freely in their communities safe from harassment and sexual assault. It's time we have a movement called "Take Back the Schools."

If we could transport chronic-behavior-problem students a couple of years into the future, then bring them back, would they better appreciate the opportunities they thumbed their noses at the first time around? Or would they not learn a thing, bringing their old ways back with them?

Since a transport system into the future has yet to be invented, the only way to see if this would work is to bring the future to them. The rules these kids love to flaunt, sometimes without repercussion, many times with repercussions they welcome or simply don't mind, are eventually going to be tested in the real world. Those students who view the world as a warm and fuzzy place where their nonsense and sass will be tolerated just like in school need to learn that that's not the way it works.

When we "understand" or put up with students who turn our classroom into a battleground, we teach them a terrible lesson. When schools allow poor behavior to continue, with only a suspension here and a reprimand there, students learn that that's how life works. They learn that the consequences for their disrespectful, "in your face" attitudes are no "biggies" and nothing to be feared. What they need to learn is that life is a series of choices, and all choices have consequences: some good, some bad, and some stunningly bad. It may be politically correct and the educational "in thing" to do, but real life doesn't work that way. The quicker you can burst this illusion bubble, the quicker you can get them back on track, fully appreciating the fact that school is a privilege, a stepping stone to a more prosperous and happy future.

In the movie *1776*, future president John Adams, when advocating independence, cried, "Good God, what are we waiting for?" Up to this point no one has pointed out to these students where their poor behavior is leading them. They believe, because we coddle them and make ill-conceived attempts to straighten them out, that all their disruptions and attention-seeking performances have no lasting consequences that they can't endure, can just laugh off, or can wear as a badge of defiance. We, as teachers, administrators, board members, and parents, are largely responsible for this mess because we have allowed it to continue far too long.

Here it is in a nutshell: an idea from Michael Goldstein, founder of the Match Charter Public High School in Boston, with a few touches added to give it a Miller flavor.

As of this writing, it costs about $11,000 per student per year for an education. A whole lot of that money is being wasted on students who have no desire to be in school and shouldn't be in school, at least at this time. Why keep them there and permit them to rob other students of a quality education? Why not put taxpayer money into an interest-bearing account for up to two years, at which time or before, those kids who have been determined "temporarily incorrigible" may return to a regular or alternative education program, determined by you and your administration? The money is there for the school if and when they return.

These students think they can make it on the "outside" with little education and no diploma? It's time they find out for themselves. Let them have the experience of going through life for a while on their own. Let them taste what it's like to be poor and struggling. Let them see how their poor attitude and I-know-everything cockiness plays in the real world. This is a "hot stove" moment they won't learn from a book, a barking teacher, or a frustrated parent begging them to straighten out for their own good.

Chances are, those who do return will be far better, more appreciative students. Those who don't return weren't about to change no matter what. School is not for everybody. It should be viewed as a privilege, not an entitlement.

Case in point: This story is so important I'm going to tell it again. Kyle was twenty years old when he came back from a two-year, self-imposed hiatus from high school. He was frustrated with life and couldn't find his place in it. A baby out of wedlock only complicated matters. He couldn't keep a job. He felt he was at the bottom of the heap. He told me point-blank during one of our first private conversations, "I was a real jerk in high school. Drugs, alcohol, disrespect. No one could tell me anything. I promise I won't cause you any problems. I want to get my high school diploma by my twenty-first birthday."

I asked him why it was so important for him to get his diploma.

"There's nothing out there without it. I'd just like to shake some of these kids," he said as he scanned the adjacent room full of students who thought they already knew everything about life. "They have no idea what it's like."

It's time to give some of these "rebels without a cause" that experience, for everyone's sake.

OBSERVATIONS

- When we push along students who have no business being promoted to the next grade until we push them right out the door, diploma in hand, we've done nothing more than produce a dysfunctional graduate.
- Do we really think the future of the country rests entirely on bringing along, at great expense and dubious results, those students who have chosen to be left behind?
- How many more vulnerable kids must be led down the wrong path by other students who have an "I don't give a crap and you can't make me" attitude? Until we face the reality that good kids who see education as a way up and out should have more influence on other kids than kids who are intent on dragging everyone around them down, nothing is going to change. To pretend otherwise is folly.
- By dumbing-down our schools and our expectations, we're producing generation after generation of Americans who can't form an independent thought or function on their own, and who have very little hope of successfully functioning in the real world. Good numbers are always impressive, but in this case, they are hollow. Hollow numbers have a way of coming back to haunt you.
- "Experience is a brutal teacher. But you learn. My God, do you learn." — C. S. Lewis, author
- To all those who get hysterical over kids losing a year of school, I ask you this: Do you want to invest a year now to get them straightened out, or do you want them to limp through the next fifty?
- If some of these kids cared to take a look, they'd realize their future is clearly visible.

- Every once in a while we need a major setback to shake up and rearrange our priorities.
- Some kids are solely focused on today and will worry about the future when they get there.
- We can't be successful if we refuse to aggressively go after anything and anyone who is blocking that success. The days of sending incorrigible students who have consistently demonstrated a disdain for the educational process to the principal's office or suspending them for a period of time, only to bring them back more emboldened than ever, must end. This catch-and-release philosophy needs to be retired and replaced with some passionate anger.
- The primary objective must be to educate and prepare as many students as possible for the hardships and rigors as well as the rewards and opportunities the real world offers. The students who have chosen, for whatever reason, to interfere with this prime directive must be separated and refocused. To continue to coddle them does no one any good, especially them.

Chapter Thirty-Four

Cut the Bull . . .

For Bobby, the favorite target of the local bullies, school had become a living hell. The fear and self-loathing had reached the point of unbearable. Each day promised yet another bottomless black hole of his existence.

He reconciled himself to accepting his second-class status as if he were somehow less than human and therefore deserving of the daily harassment. He wondered why his teachers stood idly by. Did they perhaps look upon him as deserving of this pain also? For several days in a row he was held down by the bigger boys on the school bus and forced to ride it to the end of the route, which meant he had to walk several miles to get home. The low self-esteem and depression caused suicidal thoughts, which only made it worse.

His life became about surviving and escaping. His parents reassured him that this was nothing more than a rite of passage. All kids go through this. His dad told him it would build character.

As his grades dropped, his parents jumped on the bullying bandwagon, pounding him relentlessly as a whiner and a bad student. "You're just plain weird!" his dad told him one day. He started to believe it.

The principal once suggested, with a wink and a nod, he should stand up for himself. The one time he did, in the form of a swift kick to a bully's shin, he was punished for fighting. The cruelest part was when one counselor labeled *him* a bully and suggested to his parents that anger management would be in order. That's the last time he reached out to anyone for help. It was so clear that no one had any idea what his life was like. They didn't care. He felt so alone. His life sucked.

He started the countdown to his sixteenth birthday, when he could drop out of school. But four more years was just too long to wait to escape the torment and daily humiliation that this life had to offer. With tears in his eyes, he sat down at his desk and wrote the following:

"I hope whoever reads this seeks help. I pray it's available for you. It wasn't for me. I've tried, but I simply cannot go on. I've tried to overcome the depression, shame, and outrage of bullying people. Please forgive me."

Bobby rose and headed to his closet, where one of his dad's ties would give him the relief he so desperately wanted.

The above is a compilation of actual accounts from targets of bullies.

Bullying. It's like a staph infection that invades even the most well-scrubbed hospital. It's there, lurking and ready to make someone's life miserable. But what exactly is bullying? In simplest terms, bullying is harassment, which is any verbal hostility or physical abuse of another person because of race, religion, age, gender, disability, sexual orientation, or any other legally protected status.

It is a conscious desire to cause stress in someone who is less powerful than you, to deprive someone else of a feeling of security and self-worth.

Several questions must be asked and answered before we come to any conclusions as to what to do about bullying:

Q: Is bullying really that big of a problem?

A: An estimated 160,000 children miss school every day due to fear of attack or intimidation by other students, according to the National Education Association. Anytime a child contemplates suicide or plots revenge upon his or her tormentor, or becomes depressed and so anxiety-ridden that the quality of life once enjoyed seems like a distant memory with no relief in sight, or commits suicide, it's a problem! It's a problem whether it is happening to one kid or a billion and one kids.

Q: Who needs to take responsibility?

A: We all do—each and every one of us who turns a blind eye to a child who obviously is in distress. Anyone who has any decency would never walk by a kid in pain without not only offering assistance but also actually doing something to help.

Q: Who are the bullies and why do they do it?

A: The bullies are people who are in desperate need of help themselves. When meanness toward others becomes a form of entertainment, when cruelty toward others becomes an acceptable way for a kid to spend time, you have a kid in need of professional intervention. Get them help! Punishment is not going to get them to change their ways! These kids are not born; they're created and left to flourish when we do nothing to constructively change their mindset.

Q: Can any kid become a bully?

A: Absolutely. We have all been bullies at one time or the other. And we have all been targets of bullies at some point in time. They come in all shapes and sizes. Big bullies and pint-size bullies; smart bullies and not-so-smart bullies; quiet bullies and obnoxious bullies; girl bullies and boy bullies; bullies who roam in gangs; reluctant bullies who join those groups to keep from being a target themselves; parent bullies and sibling bullies; teacher bullies and principal bullies; cyber bullies and bullies in training. In short, if you're living and breathing, you may be or used to be a bully.

Q: Are bullies ever remorseful?

A: Sure. At times, we all do things we wish we could undo, say things we'd like to take back. But herein lies the difference. Like smokers who feel regret for their filthy habit and vow not to light another one up, they do anyway. Bullying has a way of elevating one in one's own mind. Sometimes it's comforting to believe someone else is worse off than you.

Q: Do bullies have low self-esteem?

A: This common misconception has been around forever. Can they have low self-esteem? Sure. Can they think highly of themselves? Sure. They can have every other esteem in between those two. It doesn't matter. It doesn't make one iota of a difference. If they are inflicting pain and it gives them instant gratification, they are bullies.

Q: Is bullying ever beneficial?

A: Man's inhumanity to man presents an opportunity for great lessons to be learned. Look at it this way. There is no way a parent can control what someone else does or says. They only have control over themselves and their own child, and that, sometimes, is tenuous at best. It's not what you're called, but what you answer to that defines who you are. Since it is rarely clear why someone would resort to making someone else uncomfortable, it is clear that we are never going to stop it and are just tilting at windmills to think otherwise.

Does it mean we just sit back and do nothing? Of course not. It's time for a lesson with every child/student about the inner workings of a bully. This should be taught in every school, elementary through high school, to every kid. No exceptions. That is the only way we will reach all the bullies and all the targets. Here is the lesson for younger kids:

Sometimes life is not fair. Sometimes, for many different reasons, some kids pick on other kids. We all do that from time to time. Can anyone give me an example? It doesn't mean that some kids are good and some kids are bad. It simply means some kids have things going on in their lives that only they know about. And sometimes these things aren't very pleasant.

Can anyone give me an example of why some kids may be mean or bad? Do you know what? Sometimes these kids who are picking on you don't like themselves very much. Sometimes they're sad, or hurting. Sometimes they're being bullied themselves and are taking it out on you. They could really use some help. What do you think you could do to help these kids? Do you know what I would do? I'd tell someone, maybe a parent and/or a teacher or someone you really trust that this boy/girl is really acting mean and you would like to help them get some help. It must be awful being mean all the time. Isn't it more fun to be happy than to be mean?

Bullying can begin at a young age, usually by grade school or before. It must be addressed immediately by those trained to do so. Unfortunately, they can't do that if they don't know what's going on. A kid can wrap his or her head around the idea of getting help for someone else. This is where it has to be caught and addressed, because if it's not, the bullies begin to dot your middle and high schools.

Q: Who are the targets?

A: I've read the following descriptions for targets of bullies: shy loners, weaklings, sensitive kids, nerds, emotional, caring, unlikable, self-reliant, and on and on and on. Here's Miller's definition of a target of bullies: *anyone available who poses little risk of retaliation.* Ask yourself this question: Would bullies pick on kids they thought could and would retaliate without thinking twice about it?

Case in point: Missy's life took a turn for the worse during her freshman year. An intelligent girl with looks to match, she never suspected that combination would lead to so much torment from her "friends" from middle school that she started to doubt herself and who she was.

The downfall began at a party where one of the boys, a popular student, decided she was fair game and took sexual liberties despite her attempts to stop him. Distraught, she reported the abuse to her parents and school officials.

She never suspected that would be the beginning of the end for her days in that school. According to her now former friends, Joe was a swell guy and she just wrecked his life. She was shunned (quiet bullying), gossiped about, and made to look like a slut. Finally, one day, she cracked, punching one of her tormentors in the mouth during a confrontation in, of all places, the school office. The other girl suffered a cut lip and a broken tooth. The police were called. Missy was arrested for assault.

What's wrong with this picture? Why should a fifteen-year-old girl be forced to take matters into her own hands? Where were the adults? Where was someone, anyone, she could go to that actually knew what to do? The sympathy went to the other girls. They remained in school. And Missy? She was transferred to another school to maintain the peace. This scenario plays out over and over in schools today.

SO WHAT DO WE DO ABOUT IT?

To answer that question, we must first get some terms straight. The targets of bullies are targets, not victims. The term *victim* implies that the person has no power and is waiting for someone else to fix the situation. That is not always the case. The targets of bullies often do try to resolve the situation by telling others—but we don't always notice or listen. Consequently, they do feel alone and don't know where to turn next. That's where we come in.

Each school, if an effective and successful program has not been put in place, should have a task force made up of peers and trained faculty who become a much-needed oasis and support for those kids who've become targets. No, we can't leave it up to parents/guardians to handle it (sure, they should be informed), simply because they're not trained to do so. This peer support group, mentored by staff members who have the desire and training to analyze and intervene if necessary, provides a listening ear. They ascertain the nature of the situation and can notify school administrators.

The administrators and adult members of the task force can review any data about the students, including truancy, grades, and general comments from teachers, and then can notify the parents of targets and the parents of those who have chosen to target someone that the school has a zero-tolerance policy for bullying (identifying actual bullying is not an exact science, which is why staff who have been highly trained need to make the call), that the first phase of intervention has begun, and that their input and assistance is needed. Remember, sometimes what is triggering targeting behavior is coming not from within the four walls of a school but from within the four walls at home. Explain that this situation must stop now, for everyone's sake.

Case in point: The following is from an actual report from a student I had in class who wanted to relate his own story after watching a movie on bullying for a health class. I'm copying here verbatim. The names of the actual students have been changed, as they have throughout the book.

> We were made fun of for being "goth," "emo," angry," and "scary." Unlike Trevor (a kid in the movie), we didn't do anything bad to get our reputation. We just didn't talk to everyone we saw in the hallway, we weren't loud and obnoxious, and we listened to rock and screamo instead of pop or techno or rap or club music. Simply put, we were different. And apparently people don't take kindly to different. Just like the Trogs in the movie, my group was pushed around . . . literally. We were shoved into lockers, pushed into chalkboards and walls, dumped into toilets and trash cans, and ridiculed mercilessly.
>
> It got to the point where we would sit in the woods—between our school and the nearby housing complex—after school and just scream. My buddy, James, his hands were always bleeding and raw because he would punch the trees pretending they were the faces of the people who had tripped, teased, or hit him during school that day. Most of us were dealing with family issues, too, like parents coming home from Iraq, parents going over to Iraq, and all kinds of abuse. It was all just too much for us to handle . . . too much for any kid to handle. And we all felt the same way. We thought, "Well, our family doesn't want me. Society doesn't want me. Nobody wants me. So, why am I still here?"
>
> I had friends run away, not telling me where they went, and showing up weeks later looking like crap. No one took care of us, so we had to take care of each other. But no matter how many friends you have to support you, you still need an outlet. Some of us, like Paris and Jake (two more kids in the movie), resorted to cutting. Gary and Nan attempted suicide multiple times. Kathy vandalized everything in her sight. Mary and Lon went to drugs and alcohol. Bobbie, Jon, Penny, Jen, and Alice and I turned to music to comfort us. We made a band. We were good and even got a few gigs. That is until people from school, "normal" people, found out. They'd show up to wherever our gig was and throw stuff at us. Paper, pencils, paint, food, whatever they could get their hands on.
>
> Also, like Trevor (a kid in the movie), we threatened people. We never went public like he did, though, but we'd sit in the woods and say, "God, I swear, if one more person pushes me or something stupid I'm going to put a bullet in them!" or "I hate this school! I'm going to burn it to the ground one day!" I never took it seriously until Dave brought a lighter and some matches to school. As soon as he showed me those things, a billion thoughts rushed through my mind. The whole group would be blamed. He could be put in jail! People could die.

This is a serious problem, folks. It goes on right in front of us and we say, "I don't want to see that again," and fool ourselves into believing we actually did our part. We didn't. It goes on out of our sight. But it does go on, in every school, K–12, in every district in the country.

I tell grade-school kids I have only two rules when I'm in front of them. Rule #1: whenever I'm talking, you stop talking and listen. And Rule #2: never forget Rule #1. I know it has been around forever. But it always gets a laugh.

I'm not going for laughs here. Rule #1: whenever a child, regardless of age, reports they are being harassed, or says nothing and you suspect something is not right, *do something about it now, not later.* And Rule #2, never forget Rule #1.

~

OBSERVATIONS

- When students really believe in themselves, they don't have to bring other people down.
- Kids are looking at each other as reference points. Get problem students away from other problem students, put them in an advanced-placement class, and they may flounder academically, but I'll lay dollars to donuts their behavior improves dramatically for two reasons: they've lost their normal feedback audience they so desperately need and the AP students won't put up with it.
- When consequences become acceptable, they are no longer consequences, merely inconveniences. And, at some point, not even that.

Chapter Thirty-Five

United We Stand

They walk into your classroom and gather, two and three and four at a time, talking and shoving one another until the bell rings, and then reluctantly take their seat after you bark at them for the umpteenth time this semester. Then they continue to "feed" off each other, talking and disturbing the rest of the students as you try to do what you are there to do: teach.

It has become a daily ritual for these students, viewing your classroom as nothing more than a playground, a respite from their other classes where this type of anarchy is not tolerated. They play games on their laptops, glance down once in a while to text or receive one, continue chatting among themselves, seemingly oblivious to anyone else in the room, especially you.

You have already tried separating them because that is what the "classroom management" manual says will be effective. A trip to the principal's office is basically useless because they don't know what to do about these kids, and then they come strolling back into your classroom the next day, more emboldened than ever to disrupt. You're at your wit's end. What to do?

This scene plays out every day in every school in the country. Some classrooms have become nothing more than social gathering spots where the rules of the school hold no sway since they are rarely enforced in any meaningful way. Ignoring you has become a way of life and disrespecting the other students' opportunity to listen to what you have to say, uninterrupted, is of no concern to these types of kids.

Does this sound familiar?

Who are these kids? What are they hoping to accomplish? Why do they act like this? How do you deal with them?

Before we answer those questions, let's clarify two very important facts:

1. Students who gather in classrooms to "clown around" and openly defy you and basically make a pain in the butt of themselves are well aware of how disruptive their poor behavior is, and they don't care! It's a conscious choice they are making and a premeditated plan to carry out as they please in your room. It's just plain rude!

2. Just as big businesses are nothing more than a bunch of smaller businesses strung together, groups of disruptive kids are nothing more than individual kids bonded together for a common cause: to thumb their collective noses at your rules.

This book helps you to understand and deal with all kids. Well, these kids are all kids!

In the classic movie *Butch Cassidy and the Sundance Kid*, while being tracked down by the good guys, Butch turns to Sundance and says, "Who are these guys?"

Let me explain who these "guys" are.

These are kids who have probably been doing this since elementary school because someone in authority chose not to nip it in the bud then and there. When nothing of any "scary" significance happens in grade school, these kids take their act to middle school, where it takes on a life of its own. If not checked there, look out high school: here they come!

It has become the norm for one simple reason: these students have come to realize that the school will not impose any consequences of any significance on them. In effect, the school has made its own conscious choice to deal with cliques of kids who have placed their own satisfaction above everyone else's by tossing these kids back to the teacher to deal with.

Now they become your problem to deal with all over again.

They don't respect your authority because they have learned not to respect anyone's authority over them—including at home. There is a good chance you have been caught up in all this acquiescence to disrespectful behavior and maybe have not displayed any backbone yourself.

When you don't take ownership of your room immediately, you unwittingly relinquish control. But it's never too late to take it back. It may be more difficult the longer it goes unaddressed, but never too late. A good thing to remember.

The kids who form groups to disrupt a classroom are the same kids who disturb a movie-going audience because—well, because they can. They are the same kids who throw a bottle at a sports event because the call didn't go their team's way. Your classroom and your school are just another venue for this type of rude behavior.

They become annoying by their tenacity to put their own self-interest above every other kid's in your classroom. But here's the key to who they are: they are just kids pushing the envelope until someone in authority pushes back harder.

Unlike the lone troublemaker in your class who feeds on having a captive audience of peers, this faction of disruptive students already has their own reliable audience: each other.

They encourage each other to act out with a wink or a nod. And when the other students don't challenge them to stop it, they take that as a green light to continue their performance. Understand the other kids may not speak up because they may be intimidated by the sheer number of students involved or maybe even feel it's not their place. You must speak up for them.

No group of students has the right to rob the other kids of their education.

Many of these students who seek comfort in groups are insecure. As members of a "clique," their confidence expands and they can become bolder in their defiance. It's the old "strength in numbers" thing. It's the major reason students will attempt things in the presence of their group they would never think of doing on their own.

If you isolated each of these kids and had a one on one, talking to them individually, you'd probably find each less cocky and far more contrite. Some may even be a little embarrassed by the antics of the other members of the group.

Don't think for even one moment that the other kids in class are on these kids' side just because they silently endure the constant disruption. Maybe they are a bit afraid of them. When you do nothing, they suffer. In fact, some students may avoid coming to school because these groups of students have taken over and caused so much havoc.

How important is it to take back your classroom from these "cliques"?

After filling in for a teacher in sixth grade and immediately taking ownership of the room, the experienced substitute was summoned over to the desk of a little girl. When he leaned down, she whispered, "Can you be our regular teacher?" He explained that her regular teacher knew far more about the subject that he ever could. She said, "You don't understand. This is the best behaved this class has been all year."

She had grown weary of a handful of students hijacking her education. Sixth grade! She addressed him one more time as she departed the classroom for her next class. "Thank you, sir."

Don't ever think taking ownership of your room is not important. So how do you go about it when a group of students insists on wresting it away from you daily?

First, slow down and take a deep breath. Dealing with groups of students who are used to entertaining themselves while in your classroom is not all that difficult. They are looking for attention from their immediate group members, and if they get attention from some other classmates, that's okay, too. If they bother others, so be it. Rude.

If attention is what they seek, attention is what you are going to give them. Each group of students consists of a leader and followers. The leader is usually quite recognizable. He is the one the others look to for approval. Once you have identified him, you now must isolate him, and then win him over.

Leaders almost always need self-verification. They need to see confirmation of their self-concept. If someone perceives them as strong they will try to live up to that image. If someone continues to treat them like a knuckle-head, they will live up to that image. It's all about perceptions, just like teaching.

Case in point: Bob and his "gang" came to school each day from different corners of town with education the furthest thing from their minds. The school had become a big play area where anything goes. The rules meant nothing. The principals did little in the way of discipline that each of these kids couldn't handle. Punishment like ISS or detention hall was regularly assigned and regularly skipped with little consequence.

They had been allowed to get away with it for so long that some teachers simply tolerated their "in your face" attitudes as a part of doing business. Kay, one of their teachers, had had enough. As class was about to be dismissed, she whispered in Bob's ear, "I need a favor to ask you. It's important and I can really use your help. Do you have a minute today?"

She also remembered the three things that are so vital when attempting to change poor behavior into acceptable behavior: (1) Always talk in terms of what the other guy wants; (2) allow them to correct themselves; and (3) always give them the feeling of being in control of things by giving them options. TV game shows use the same philosophy: do you want door number one, two, or three? That sort of thing. Magicians also use this technique when trying to sell an illusion. Have you ever noticed? Holding out two clenched fists, they say, "Pick one."

Kay took Bob by surprise. She played into his need to feel important. Anytime anyone asks you for a favor, you must have something they don't. "Is lunchtime all right?" Once again she gave him a choice, in this case, yes or no to the lunchtime offer.

As they sat down at the mutually agreed-upon time, she explained, "When you guys disrupt my class like that it not only hurts the other students' education but also makes my job a lot harder. Do you know I get evaluated each year, and my job depends on getting a good evaluation?"

She immediately took charge of the meeting and laid out what this was all about. No beating around the bush.

She was also establishing that not only were the other students being harmed by the poor behavior, but also she had a personal stake in it. People who have a "personal" stake in something are usually people who are so driven you really don't want to stand in their way. Even kids understand this concept.

He may reply "yes" or "no" or "I really don't care" just to continue his defiance. It doesn't matter how he responds. Don't hesitate; just continue taking charge using a little Psychology 101.

"Here's where I need your help. I know you're smart and I cannot quite figure out why you insist on disrupting my classes. But I do want you, as I want all the rest of the students, to pass this course, and in your case it simply is not going to happen the way things are now." Once again, they may say "why?" or "I don't care." It doesn't matter.

"Whether that's any concern to you or not I'm really not sure. But it is a concern to the vast majority of your classmates, and I have to look out for them. So here are your two options. Option number 1, which you will find far more pleasant than option number 2, is I'm going to go out of my way to help you pass this course, because if you don't, you'll have to take it over again. I'm not going to just give you a grade; you are going to have to earn it. And you'll earn it by helping the rest of your little group pass this course. In effect, what I'm proposing is you will become my assistant during the class with your buddies, which means you are going to have to know this subject. I think you have what it takes. Do you?"

Remember this rule: once you ask a question of a student, *shut up!* Their answer or their lack of an answer will tell you preciously where to go from there.

Notice she didn't make the situation worse. She made him an offer that should be appealing to him, even if he had already been passing the course, because it put him in a leadership role in her class. She let him save face by having this conversation in private. And she ended it by asking him a simple question that required a yes or no answer.

Kay was playing up to his ego. If he declines the offer, he has admitted he doesn't have what it takes. No kid who thinks he's a leader wants to believe he doesn't have the "right stuff." She in effect has given him a fine reputation to live up to.

You as the teacher don't have the time or perhaps the skills to deal with three or four out-of-control students at once. But Bob does. Win him over and the rest of this little clique will fall in line.

She took charge of the situation and she did it on her terms. She had made up her mind that this behavior needed to stop for everyone's sake. She remained calm and displayed self-assurance. She was resolute in her desire to bring this thing to an end, and it came across that way. She made sure Bob noticed.

If he agrees, have a plan in place starting with the next class. Thank him for his cooperation and tell him you look forward to "working" with him.

If he asks what option number 2 would have been, simply inform him that you are glad it didn't come to that because it's an option you try to avoid because even you find it unpleasant and you'll keep it to yourself.

And option number 2? That's up to you. It depends on school policy. It may be this class is over for you this semester.

Or he will be taking this class in ISS for the remainder of the semester. Or anything else that may be unappealing to a leader. But try option number 1 first. If it doesn't work out, you have left yourself options.

To recap. Leaders have egos. Play up to that ego. You want to win this kid over because if you do the rest of his group falls in line. Never threaten punishment if he doesn't quit disrupting your class. That often causes a kid like this to dig in even further. Give him choices to give him the "illusion" he has some control over the outcome.

And what's the most important thing you need to accomplish during this little meeting? You need to show him you are a genuinely good person. It is the perfect opportunity for you to get him to buy into you as someone who has his best interest at heart.

Following these basic commonsense principles should help you deal more effectively with groups of students who have become a daily annoyance in your classroom.

Chapter Thirty-Six

Alternative Schools

When an alternative education program is properly administered and staffed with highly trained and experienced faculty, it can be a valuable asset not only to your school but also to the students who have been placed there. It should provide an opportunity for growth and the direction needed to maximize their abilities.

Even with a decade of experience dealing with "at-risk" students, I wanted to verify my findings and conclusions with a leading authority in this field before I shared advice on how to run a successful alternative education school.

Many thanks to Dr. Steve Laidacker, executive director of the Lakeside Academy (operated by Sequel Youth and Family Services) in Kalamazoo, Michigan, for generously sharing his time and expertise with me. With his permission, Dr. Laidacker is quoted throughout this chapter.

If you are going to start or revamp an alternative education school in your district, you must answer three questions before you proceed. If you can't answer these questions honestly or are not sure how to answer them, you should hold off on this idea until you are absolutely sure of your school's goals in starting or continuing an alternative education program.

Here they are: (1) What does your school hope to accomplish with an alternative education program? (2) What are you willing to do to make it happen? (3) Will it make a positive impact on these young lives?

But first things first.

The subtitle of this book is "Taking Custody of Your Classroom." The majority of students who will be placed in your alternative school will be the kids who have discipline and emotion issues and are probably, in most cases, the students who are disrupting your classrooms and schools. The reasons for this are myriad, as we have discussed.

Most of these students will eventually be mainstreamed back into regular education classes at some point. If your alternative school is run properly by a highly trained and dedicated staff, the goal is to show these struggling kids there is a better way to behave and get them to start believing in themselves again so when they return to regular education, they will be far less disruptive.

If you are using your alternative school as nothing more than a warehouse and a day care center for wayward teens, it will be self-defeating. An excellent opportunity to straighten out these students will have been lost and may not present itself again.

These young lives are often spiraling out of control, and I have discovered over the past decade of dealing with "at-risk" kids that well-intentioned but ill-prepared people oftentimes not only don't help these kids but also inadvertently cripple them in the process.

You see, no matter how lofty your intentions are, sometimes people who start and run these schools have little or no knowledge of what makes this type of student "tick," incorrectly assuming all students are basically the same and will respond to the same stimuli as all the other students. It is one of the biggest faulty assumptions.

Another faulty assumption is that any teacher who is available is a good choice for a teaching position. Nothing could be further from the truth. We will discuss this faulty assumption and many more as we move on.

Administrators and counselors who may have all the right credentials oftentimes step into unknown territory and rely solely on those credentials to put them into the "I know more than everyone else" category. When somebody feels they have nothing to learn from someone else because of their perceived lofty status, bad things usually happen. Therefore, sound planning and open communication are necessary for an alternative school to flourish.

But let's go back a few steps. The beginning of the alternative education movement can be traced to the earliest days of our country. Somehow, they knew back then that all kids can't be expected to learn at the same rate. It doesn't mean they can't learn; it simply means they may need a little more help and a little more time to grasp ideas. Or they may have other problems that are not being addressed.

Or maybe, God forbid, regular education isn't for every kid for many reasons. But with all the hobbling laws and mandates put in place by our leaders who apparently think every kid is going to be a rocket scientist or brain surgeon, maybe it is blasphemous for me to say such things! So be it.

And yet we, by our own making, have produced the atmosphere ripe with the need for alternative schools when we insist education be timed with a stop watch. The more kids we can waltz across the stage at the magic age of eighteen, the more we pat ourselves on the back and fool ourselves into believing what a great job we have done as educators.

We promote kids who have fallen so far behind the other kids, sometimes for the simplest of reasons; we never gave them the tools necessary *not* to fall behind! (Refer to chapter 30, "Thanks for the Memory.") But because we don't want to damage their psyches or some other nonsense, we send them on their way grade after grade. We develop summer schools and credit recovery programs that are little more than gimmicks to get these kids off that stage at eighteen, diploma in hand, only to disappear at the end of the ceremony.

Some kids who balk because they are truly troubled and lost and cause all kinds of havoc in a school need to be some place other than a regular classroom. Hello alternative education. The thinking goes: get them away from the other students so those kids have a better chance of succeeding in school. Separate the bad influences or the kids ready to drop out from the kids who maybe, just maybe, have a chance at success, and we have a win-win situation.

These "in-school" dropouts are often treated as throw-away kids. They are not throw-away kids! They are not disposable people to be locked away. They oftentimes have issues and problems that are not being dealt with. Some are lost and drifting aimlessly. What some of them need more than anything is a caring adult in whom they can truly believe.

They sorely need a grownup they can trust who will take the place of the father or mother they never knew or wish they had never known. When any one of these kids feels there is no adult out there they can rely on, when these kids have a sense they don't matter anymore, you have an alternative education student in waiting.

They need someone in authority to say to them, "I'm here and I care. You can count on me."

If you knew what some of these young people have had to endure during their short lifetimes, you would wonder how they got this far. If you or I had the same life experiences they had, we would probably be candidates for an alternative school.

I'm not trying to make excuses for these kids. I am trying to explain why some end up in an alternative school. Every student, including the most disruptive kid, has the right to an opportunity for a good education. What they don't have, and never should have, is a continuing opportunity to derail other students' opportunity to learn.

I am also not trying to dissuade you from starting a new alternative school. A properly run and goal-oriented alternative program can and should be a big plus for any school. I simply want you to understand before you dive head-first into initiating an alternative school in your district that it is not as easy as it looks.

Anyone who wants to be involved in running a successful alternative school must meet definite standards. And a successful school is one that prepares these kids to carry on without us. It instills a sense of self-worth so lacking in a lot of these kids and gives them a vision of a bright and hopeful future.

It not only provides the tools necessary for students to learn, but also gives them the will to want to learn more.

It's a huge responsibility—one not to be taken lightly. These schools must never be allowed to become warehouses or low-functioning day care centers for wayward children, which they have often devolved into in every corner of this country

All these kids bring baggage. They are often unsure of themselves, skeptical that anyone can really be trusted or would actually want to help them. Some students have hang-ups and problems buried so deep they may never be reached.

Some have lost the will to learn, so they quit trying because it has become too painful.

Some are simply treading water and running short of air. You're the air!

Sometimes they have fooled themselves into believing they don't need any help. They are all different, and all the same. Unsure of themselves sometimes, but putting up a good front all the time. They don't trust you and, in their own minds, have every reason to feel that way.

There is only one thing they are all absolutely sure of: how they feel.

We are going to use that one absolute as we learn to deal with these kids so they can have a better chance to succeed in school and in life.

In short, if you are going to do something, make it matter!

Let us begin.

WHY YOU AND THEY ARE HERE

It is vital that your core faculty members know precisely why each student has been assigned to alternative education. Is it because he is continually truant? Is she disrespectful to the teachers? What kind of grades is he getting? Is she flunking any subject(s)? What subjects? Does he have a drug problem? Is it a weapons offense? Has he been identified as a bully? Is she on probation? For what offense? Who's her probation officer? (I'll explain why later.) Is going to school a requirement of probation? Or did he do something dumb like bring a can of beer into school on a dare?

Whatever the reason is, it is important the staff knows the circumstances of each student's assignment and the student's track record in school in order to effectively and intelligently structure a game plan to help this student. Keeping staff in the dark because of the Federal Educational Rights and Privacy Act (FERPA) is a gross misinterpretation of that law and hinders your staff's performance.

FERPA is based on the HIPAA Privacy Rule. 34 CFR, Part 99, Section 99.31 (1) (i) (A) reads, concerning school officials:

Under current regulations, school districts and postsecondary institutions may allow "school officials, including teachers, within the agency or institution" to have access to students' educational records, without consent, if they have determined that the official has legitimate educational interests in the information.

An educational record is any record that contains information directly related to a student that is maintained by the institution. This includes, but is not limited to, grade information, disciplinary documentation, and billing and financial aid data.

> HIPPA, on which FERPA is based, is the singular more misapplied, misunderstood piece of federal legislation ever created, other than the tax code. It is often incorrectly applied. There is significant information that teachers need in order to be effective and to help that student be safe. FERPA does not restrict that information.
> Those administrators who hide behind FERPA are often misinformed, or sometimes taking the easy way out. (Dr. Laidacker)

One of the worst things any school can do is bring in a parade of new teachers throughout the year who have little or no background or experience in dealing with this student population. It can be a recipe for disaster. And yet, when people are put in charge of alternative schools with those "right credentials and I know more than anyone else" attitudes, this common mistake is often perpetrated to the detriment of both the student population and the cohesiveness of the staff, which is of paramount importance.

Often, these kids already come in with a poor attitude toward school and a skewered outlook on life and authority figures. Their trust of adults may be at a low point in their lives. They need consistency in order to have any chance of restoring that trust, which is vital if you ever want to reach them.

Remember, a lot of these kids feel like they don't matter to anyone, so why even try? Bring inexperienced staff into the mix, whether they are new to the profession or veteran teachers who have never been properly trained to deal with this type of student, and you have said to the students, in effect, "You really don't matter to us. That is why we are going to let anyone who signs up to be on the staff to get in some hours."

These kids may be disruptive, but they are not dumb. They pick up on these types of things quickly. Stop selling them short!

Your staff must be a small core of highly trained and experienced educators dedicated to helping these "throw-away" kids. Everybody has to be on the same page, on the same mission, and that mission is to show these students that it doesn't have to be this way. They have to trust you when you say to them, "We can turn this thing around."

If you insist on staffing your alternative program with a large pool of inexperienced people, it is quite possibly designed for failure.

> The first thing you must understand when starting up an alternative education program, it's not going to be about the student. It's going to be about the structure and the staff. You need an administration in place that will not attempt the path of a traditional public school when it comes to discipline, etc. With the public school perspective on education, there's a good chance it won't match the student's actual needs.
>
> When starting an alternative program, if the union, for example, is going to dictate what teachers you are going to get, it's often doomed for failure. (Dr. Laidacker)

The staffing of a successful alternative program starts from the top down. If you are going to assign the new assistant principal who recently got his certificate as the person in charge just because he is the low person on the totem pole, or the first-year teacher who majored in psychology or sociology but has no real day-to-day experience with these types of kids, relying only on what she learned in college or on the Internet, forget about it.

The person in charge needs to be a leader whom the staff and the students can and want to respect. This person needs to be in the alternative school the vast majority of the days and be able to listen to and work with the core staff. In fact, this person should have the biggest hand in hiring this staff.

The person in charge should have the capacity and willingness to listen attentively to the staff regarding what needs to be done to keep things running as smoothly as possible or what needs to be accomplished to right the ship. This person should not come in thinking he or she has all the answers, because no one does. Many failed leaders never grasp this concept.

If you have such a person, hire them. If you don't, keep looking. It's that important.

Please note, an absentee figurehead who shows up now and again only to issue dictates and unenforceable mandates on how things should happen in the school is sheer nonsense and a real good way to destroy any type of unity and bonding between staff and students.

> When I am hiring a teacher, I ask, "What do you do if a kid says, f**k you!" If they give an answer such as "I will remind them that we do not use that type of language here" or "I don't know," I may ask them the same question a second and third time. If they finally say, send them to the principal's office, that interview is over, that applicant can leave. They're not hired.
>
> A huge mistake and the singularly worst quote is a teacher uttering: "I'll show them respect when they show me respect." It's very frustrating to hear this. Most students who end up in alternative education will test a teacher dozens, even hundreds of times. It's up to the adult to demonstrate respect every single

time until a relationship begins to form and until a student feels comfortable demonstrating respect back.

It's like an emotional bank account. You are going to have to make a whole lot of deposits until you can make a withdrawal. (Dr. Laidacker)

Unfortunately with all the laws and mandates passed by misguided bureaucrats, alternative education schools have, at times, descended into being nothing more than dumping grounds for disruptive youth. The thinking goes this way: get them out of the regular education classes—because the teachers and administrators are tired of dealing with them day in and day out—and things will calm down around here.

But you can't throw them out of school because it will prove too costly for your district. If just ten of these kids chose to go the cyber school route, it would put a huge hole in the district wallet! You see, the state mandates that these kids are provided with an education, whether in your brick-and-mortar building or elsewhere. The only sure thing is your district is going to pay for it, one way or another.

This is why I use the term *dumping grounds*. When kids are enrolled in an alternative school and really don't want to be there, or in any school for that matter, students who are openly defiant and not above terrorizing other students and their teachers, you are inviting problems for your alternative staff who are already up to their necks with other problem kids.

You are inviting these kids to come over from regular education to drag down and be a poor influence on students your staff is trying to turn around. It's vital these "struggling and lost and acting out with abandon" students realize and accept before this placement that it is for their own well-being. They must demonstrate to the interviewing staff, which may consist of the entire faculty or a representative group, and to their parents/guardians, that alternative education is the way to go at this time.

We have face-to-face interviews. We don't accept everyone. They must want some level of assistance and help. We know why they are here.

It's probably not necessary to have the entire staff in on every interview. You may want to rotate the faculty.

Ask them during the interview: Do they have a diagnosis that is going to impact their education? Do they have charges that are going to impact their education? Do they have any affiliation with any student here that might impact their education?

Don't accept a kid into the program until you have this interview with them. Interview him/her privately, and then bring in the parents.

Don't talk about the running of the school. Talk about the specific education of that student. From the interview, you'll get all the information you want. (Dr. Laidacker)

A LOOK AT DISCIPLINE

In-school and out-of-school suspensions, along with after-school detention halls, have become such a way of life today in just about all districts in this country as a means of "punishing" students into better behavior that I almost hesitate to venture onto this hallowed ground.

Suspensions and detention halls don't work. They don't accomplish what they are intended to accomplish! Take a look at a list of all the kids who have been "assigned" to one of these punishments in a regular public school and guess what you'll come up with. The same names over and over again! That should be your first clue that these archaic practices, as they are presently instituted, do nothing but waste everyone's time and patience.

So why are they still the last resort of most schools and administrators? Because this is all they have left to fall back on when all else fails. The question that must be proposed is this: why has all else failed? I have attempted to answer that question throughout this book.

Another question: Do you want to punish these kids, or do you want to change poor behavior into acceptable behavior? Do you really believe this consequence is going to change this kid? Take a look at that list of names again.

When consequences become acceptable, they are no longer consequences. They are merely inconveniences. At some point, they are not even that. Consequences meted out to each and every kid for the same infraction, as if all students are nothing more than mindless robots, is a cop-out.

Eventually, this parade of students into your ISS or detention halls, or that kid who gets tossed out of school for the umpteenth time, will make their way, with your blessing, over to your alternative education school. They have not been corrected because someone has not taken the time or doesn't know how to make that correction successfully.

So what's left? Suspension and detention. The old standbys that don't intelligently deal with the unwanted behavior of these students; they simply postpone it for another day, to be "dealt with" all over again when the students return to regular classes. Sometimes they even come back as a hero to some of the more impressionable kids!

It's a pattern that needs to be revamped or eliminated altogether. The best way to keep the population of an alternative school low is to address poor behavior immediately and as often as necessary when this child is in regular education. It's never too soon to begin.

I don't see ISS or detention halls being eliminated anytime soon. If nothing else, they do separate the disruptive kids from the rest of your school population for a while. But don't turn it into a party time for these students—that's what happens when you assign more than one student to a room.

If a student is assigned ISS or detention, bring in the teacher(s) who wrote him or her up, along with an administrator and guidance counselor, for a heart-to-heart meeting with this student. Explain in simple terms that the disruptive behavior is negatively affecting the other students' education. "If those other students were disrupting your education, they would be sitting right where you are sitting. We don't play favorites."

Have someone retrieve the students from their homeroom at the beginning of the day to serve ISS. Same thing if it is an after-school detention. Never let them know what day it will be. Daily class assignments from each of their teachers should be waiting for them and are to be turned into that teacher by the end of the day. If they are not completed, assign an after-school detention to complete them then and there. No exceptions.

If they miss a sports practice or game, or any other extracurricular activity, so be it. You should have already contacted the coach, instructor, and parents and explained the situation to them. It is always wise to get their buy-in on this. Remind them you know sports and extracurricular activities are important, but this takes precedence every single time. Tell them you don't feel bad about doing this; you feel bad that their player (child) made it necessary.

There will be no iPods, cell phones, or other electronic devices allowed unless they are part of the curriculum.

They will serve their time by themselves, unless a teacher is assigned to help them with their studies. No other students are to be in the room. They will not be allowed to get their own lunch; it will be brought to them. They will get scheduled bathroom breaks at the nearest facility while the rest of the student population is in class.

Please note: One of the worst things to do when students are in alternative education is to suspend them from that school. Unless it's a weapons violation or something similar, it's usually giving them exactly what they want.

We have to throw away the book for discipline. We have to keep them in school. Don't send them home to sleep until noon, eat cold pizza, and watch TV.

The reason for a consequence is to change behavior and to teach. If a consequence is issued that does not matter to a kid, but is simply used because it is written down, then the consequence is meaningless.

Teachers cannot have the latitude of simply emptying their rooms and making a parade. That being said, a student can't terrorize the school. When I ran an ISS, if I had a student who literally could not be in the classroom then they would be removed and they would be in ISS for up to ten days (or the legal limit). I did not want them to interact with other students. One of the most compelling things for students that age is social interaction. So I would try to immediately wipe out any chance they had for social interaction, including lunch time, etc.

That's a big deterrent. People often have no idea how to use ISS in the public sector. They take a kid out for a period, and then bring him back in and he goes back and forth over the day. That's a NO. For ISS to be effective, it literally has to be on the extreme side.

After-school detention may have a desired impact for normal behaviors and nuisance behaviors. I prefer it to be unannounced until the day of the detention. Don't let them know what day it's going to be because they'll take that day off. To announce it in advance that "This Thursday we are going to have after school detention"? That's just asinine. (Dr. Laidacker)

Consistency in alternative programs and in regular education is of paramount importance. Unfortunately, the meaning of *consistency* often gets twisted and misconstrued because teachers and administrators have different interpretations. This is where a lot of problems have their beginning.

One teacher allows one thing the next forbids. One administrator is a strict by-the-rulebook type of person and the assistant principal down the hall is a little more lenient because maybe he was much like some of these kids when he walked the halls of his school back in the day and can identify with them.

When schools have a distinct disconnect between faculty and administration when it comes to consistency in dealing with behavior problems, I can pretty much guarantee problems ahead—problems of your own making. This is especially true in alternative schools.

The kids placed there already have some type of discipline issue. We already know that. Why muddy the water with an inconsistent approach when dealing with unwanted behavior?

This is why it is critical to have regular team meetings to discuss strategies, student behaviors, and anything that may affect a positive outcome for these kids. Alternative school leaders can't stick their heads in the sand and pretend everything is working just fine. Rarely is everything working just fine! An alternative school that is resistant to regularly scheduled meetings and open communication between staff and administration is a school that is leaderless!

Holding weekly meetings is not unreasonable. Daily, perhaps fifteen or twenty minutes each day before school begins, is even better. It's how successful businesses do it.

There is no way everyone can be on the same page if no one feels comfortable or if nobody is given the platform to express themselves. In the movie *1776*, a representative from the state of Rhode Island, when asked if there should be an open discussion concerning independence, said, "Of course there should be! I don't know anything so dangerous it can't be talked about!" And that should apply here. Regular communication and sharing is the only way to achieve consistency of staff and a coherent approach toward a desired outcome with these kids.

Now, what does *consistency* mean?

> There seems to be an extraordinarily high level of distancing among staff. Some of these kids are here for an emotional issue instead of a learning disability. It's behavioral, not, for example, a learning disability such as dyslexia. We need an individual approach designed for the individual's needs, skills, and situation of that student or it's not going to work.
>
> What consistency is, then, is that every single thing is dealt with. It's going to be addressed and a decision is going to be made about what that student needs at that moment and the same for any others involved. It's going to be in the best interest of that student(s) and to change behavior.
>
> I'm not talking about the rules of the school and the classroom. I'm talking about an approach. If someone does something wrong, it will be addressed and it won't be ignored. Those who go only by the rule book are people who often struggle with consistency. Those teachers and administrators need to have it orderly and artificially enforced.
>
> What it's not about is being so consistent on every infraction that every consequence must be identical. What I mean by consistency is, you must approach every situation and deal with it. You must not turn your backs on it. For example, if they curse, it means you are going to address it. It doesn't mean you are going to crush the student.
>
> But that's frequently the only thing they (teachers) have left to fall back on because colleges and universities are often not preparing teachers for today's disruptive student. They are preparing them for the college prep kids and the learning disabled. They are not preparing them for the kid who is drinking beer at age fourteen or the kid who says, "f**k you, why do I need this science?"
>
> Anybody can be a master of a curriculum. That has little to do with being a good teacher. It's about building relationships and being consistent. (Dr. Laidacker)

Many of the students in your alternative school are drifting aimlessly through the day and through their lives. Their trust of authority figures is shot, oftentimes for good reason. They have thrown in the towel when it comes to education and it may even become quite comforting to do this. The pressure is off to succeed when you have embraced failure as acceptable.

They perceive that nobody at home gives a damn about them and their education, so why should they? Do you realize some kids are actually failing on purpose? It may be to get back at a parent, or it may be to fit in with a certain crowd at school.

Comedian Dennis Miller once said of kids like these, "Some have nobody who lives down the hall that they fear." I get what he was trying to say. They have nobody that they can go to whom they respect, who is there for them, unconditionally. Sometimes, nobody lives down the hall, period.

When children feel alone and abandoned, they sometimes do crazy things; they act out. They do things that would not have occurred to them to do if there were someone they felt comfortable confiding in—someone they could trust to let it all hang out with, someone with whom they could share a quiet moment to get some things off their chest.

Most of these kids have issues that are not being addressed. Parking them in a classroom to stare at a computer for hours on end is not helping those issues, nor is waiting on a "trained" counselor whom they don't know to arrive on the scene every week or so to conduct a ten-minute conversation in private.

You need a system of mentoring in alternative programs that puts the personal needs and concerns of the student on the front burner, not the back burner, each and every day.

When a student clicks with one of your alternative teachers, that teacher should become the student's confidant, mentor. That teacher needs to be there almost every day so this student can count on someone being there they can trust and confide in. This is why a small core of trained faculty is imperative.

Rotating teachers out every one or two weeks is self-defeating.

> Any program that does not have a mentoring and tutoring program in place is missing a significant opportunity. When used correctly, mentoring provides two things: it benefits the younger students and sometimes greatly benefits the older mentors. (Dr. Laidacker)

Take Ownership of the Room Immediately

Once your staff has been selected and properly educated on this type of student population, it is now time to put together a game plan.

The team must be in charge of this environment from the outset. It's the only way this works. All your good intentions will go flying out the window if you do not immediately take ownership of the room. The students need to understand and accept during the interview process that this school, this opportunity they are being offered, comes with the proviso: this is our place!

We set the agenda. We make the calls. We are going to demonstrate to the student why making better choices can lead to a happier, more productive life. The expectations you have for each student should be spelled out from the very beginning. They must be fair and purpose driven. See the list at the end of this chapter.

Keep in mind that for anyone to buy what you're selling, they must buy into you, the staff. They must understand there are rewards for good behavior and consequences for unacceptable behavior. The goal is never to punish, but to teach a lesson. Like in the real world, they will be held accountable for their actions because they are responsible for those actions.

I use the following analogy: Did you ever notice how quiet most libraries are in schools? Did you ever wonder why that is? Because librarians will have it no other way. This is their fiefdom. This is their territory. You go by their rules or you're gone. Most students adhere to this because they have been exposed to this concept since grade school. It has become acceptable to them because it is expected of them.

Even when the librarian leaves the room, the noise level remains low. You must emulate the librarian. You set the expectations at the beginning and address all infractions. You are in charge. You're the only adults in the room. Act like it!

> This is a perfect philosophy and dead on accurate. It becomes chaotic when one person has not taken ownership of the room. (Dr. Laidacker)

The bond between teacher and student cannot be overemphasized. It's the building block on which great things can happen. It can be as strong as tensile steel and as fragile as a twig, all at the same time. And it can snap in a heartbeat with just one misstep from a teacher or administrator.

Use your head! If some infraction occurs, ask yourself if this is worth starting World War III over. You see, the vast majority of time when things go south, it's the teachers themselves who caused it, or they certainly exacerbated the situation. They take a small spark, in this case a kid testing the bounds, and throw gasoline all over it. They are shocked it didn't calm things down! They then back the kid into a corner and force him to make a decision. The student can back down or double down right there.

I cannot emphasize this enough: Sometimes teachers become their own worst enemy. They paint themselves into a corner because they paint the student into a corner!

Even kids whom you think you have bonded with will push the envelope now and again. Don't make it personal! Don't get all beside yourself and do something rash. She is a kid! They do these things once in a while. Expect it.

Look at it this way. Even your best friends push your buttons sometimes. Do you hop all over them? Not if you want to remain friends. People have off days; they do stuff they wish they could undo almost as soon as they do them. So do you.

It's a kid being a kid. It's a teenager being a teenager. That's just how they are. That's just how we were when we were their age. Your reaction to their infraction sets the tone of how this thing will play out. All the other kids in the room now have their gaze pointed directly at you to see how you will handle it. Always remember that. Treat it as a teachable moment for all of them.

In regular education the above scenario plays out in every school occasionally. In alternative education it plays out much more frequently. Get used to it. It is not worth getting your blood pressure to a boil. It must be addressed and dealt with. There is no way around that. But whatever you do, make sure that a fragile bond isn't snapped, possibly for good. It takes a long time to create, and one hot-headed moment from you can take you and this kid right back to square one. Reconstructing that bond can take forever, or it may never happen again.

There are many things a teacher should want to avoid like the plague. The first thing to avoid is the knee-jerk reaction of sending this kid to the office. It conveys two things to that student: (1) you don't know how to handle this, and (2) you just ratted him out. End of bond.

The second thing to avoid is putting down a student in front of her peers. No one likes to be embarrassed, even if they know they are in the wrong. Don't blow this thing, whatever this thing is, way out of whack. It is simply not worth the price you may have to pay in your attempt to reach this kid.

> A huge mistake teachers make (if a student misbehaves in the classroom) is sending them to the office. Evidence based research shows the three worst and least effective things to do while a student is acting out is: Send them out of the room to go talk to somebody. Send them out to talk to somebody with more initials after their name. Punish them.
>
> The only one who can control the behavior in the classroom is the teacher. Only the teacher can guide and control those behaviors. Not the principal, not the guidance counselor, not the police officer or the probation officer.
>
> It's done through consistent application. It's done by genuinely being a person, not a phony. It's done by demonstrating respect repeatedly.
>
> Take the above and tie it in a bow and you're well on your way to having a successful program.
>
> When I hear any educator make the statement, "what we need around here are more consequences," what they are actually saying is, "I don't have the skills needed to deal with this particular kid's behavior. And if you can't give me those skills, then I will revert to the only other thing I know which is consequences." (Dr. Laidacker)

Leaders don't make deals. They make decisions. Those decisions should be based on what is best for everyone concerned and what is the best way to proceed in order to meet established goals.

That being said, far too many teachers, especially in alternative education, seem to go out of their way to make deals with students, especially the more disruptive ones. The thinking is this: give the kid a deal and hope he'll cooperate.

Parents who have lost control of their children and their homes often choose the same route. If you do this, Mary, you get to do this. The problem with this type of thinking, this stick-and-carrot approach, is that a larger carrot and a shorter stick are eventually needed as time goes by and the kid gets older and wiser.

It's opening a can of worms. And once you open that can, you rarely get the lid back on. It's a hole many teachers dig for themselves that almost always comes back to bite them. If you find yourself in this hole, quit digging.

This type of thing is prevalent in the alternative programs I have studied. I get it, to a point. Oftentimes the faculty is just trying to make it through the day. If a concession here or there with these kids is what it takes to accomplish that, then concession it is.

If you have a staff of inexperienced teachers who are unsure how to deal with this student population, they will most likely take this route to avoid any conflict with these kids. But, like a child who throws a temper tantrum, holding their breath and stomping their little feet on the floor until they get their way, only to throw a bigger tantrum, it will happen again. It's never a wise thing to do.

When a teacher plays "trade-off" with a student, it gives a clear signal to that kid that issuing demands and making deals is acceptable here. Whenever they don't want to do something, they start a "dialogue" with this teacher, keep after the teacher long enough, and he or she will acquiesce to the deal. They can actually get quite good at it.

Listen closely. In all schools, but especially alternative programs, you don't make deals! You are in charge. This is how the day is going to play out, for the good of everyone concerned.

To allow students to have a choice in how the day plays out when they already have a history of making poor choices is ludicrous.

> You can't be a deal maker. For example, they say I'll do my homework if I don't have to do this. Or, I know we're supposed to do the worksheet now, but I want to do this right now. If you start getting into that, THEY end up determining what the course of the day is going to look like.
> If, for instance, math time is 10:00, then that is what it is. It should not be up to the student to determine. If we specifically want to engage the students' opinion of some things and get their input on certain topics, that's fine. But once it has been determined, then it's not their call when those kinds of things occur. (Dr. Laidacker)

RULES AND POLICIES

One of the biggest debates in any school is whether the use of cell phones and iPods should be permitted. The thoughts range from "how are you going to stop them" to "these things are a major distraction and need to be banned." I'm quite sure your school falls in between these two markers.

I mention in one of my observations that if cell phones and texting are a distraction when driving, why are they not considered a distraction in school? Scientific evidence has proven that no one has the ability to do two things at once and give 100 percent to each task.

Never put a policy in place if it is unenforceable. Whenever a teacher or a school has to back down because the rules are so unpopular and far too time-consuming to enforce, it opens the flood gates to other demands from the student population.

If your school has a policy that states all cell phones and iPods remain in the locker throughout the day, make sure every and all infractions are addressed immediately. If your policy is that cell phones and iPods may be used during some other time frame during the school day, make sure you enforce those rules also.

The students need to be aware that rules put into place by schools are there for a specific reason. Explain what that reason is. They are not put in place just to make their young lives miserable! They need to understand our society is based on rules (laws) for the good of all.

This is how the real world operates. This is how businesses operate. And this is how your school operates.

> In alternative programs, it can't be any different than in regular education. Both should be the same. If they get caught using a cell phone or iPod when (or where) they know they shouldn't be, you say, "You know what the standard is, you know what the expectation is. Give me the phone and get it at the end of the day."
>
> But the bottom line is this. If they walk into the school at 8:00 with a cell phone, it's because it's a pattern that they have been ALLOWED to do in that building and in that school. It's because we didn't bother to make it important enough so that student willingly passed over the phones.
>
> We are not trying to catch them! That's not what it is. We are saying, this is our school and here are our expectations. Here is the normative culture that we are trying to create, and to do that, we are making sure everybody has a chance to maneuver through the system.
>
> This is what WE are going to agree to do. We are coming at this as a positive rather than, "I'm going to catch you with that cell phone!" That's old school thinking and in my opinion part of what is wrong in education. (Dr. Laidacker)

A friend of mine is a doctor contracted by state and federal prisons to treat inmates. He is looked upon by the inmates as a "sacred cow." He is there to help all of them with their medical problems and is untouchable inside the prison walls. In effect, all the inmates are his protectors.

The only time he has ever felt uncomfortable inside those walls is when he has had to tell them "no." They don't like being told "no" to any request they make, he informed me. So he quit telling them "no." Instead, he says, "I'm not sure. I'll look into for you," or, "That's an interesting idea. Let me run it by the people in charge," or, "I'm not really sure of the answer. I'll get back to you on it."

But he quit saying "no" to these guys! Apparently, the "sacred cow" thing has its limits.

In alternative education, you are going to deal with kids who are not used to hearing the word *no*. You are going to run into students who are used to flaunting the rules and causing problems until they get their way. It just comes with the territory.

Some of these kids have become accustomed to getting their own way. Especially in the home! So they bring this "acquired" entitlement into your school building and eventually into your alternative program.

So how do you say "no" to a kid who really doesn't like to hear the word *no*?

> No is important, but again it's a we/they thing. Adults don't have to say a lot of no's. What the adults have to do is say to the kid, "Alright, listen. Here's the issue right now. Don't tell me what you want to do. Tell me, from everything you know about us and what we talk about, what our values are and what our expectations are, what's the correct answer?" (Dr. Laidacker)

ATTENTION, PLEASE

Disruptions are a way of life in an alternative school. You usually will deal with the best kings and queens of disruptions your school has to offer! The main question that requires an answer before you will ever know the best course to deal with a disruptive student is: Why do they feel it is necessary to disrupt? Answer that, which sometimes needs some digging on your part, and you can intelligently deal with this kid.

There is always a reason why a student acts up in class. They are not born this way. Something, or someone, has caused them to go off the rails. Sometimes they themselves may not fully understand why they do what they do and are actually confused as to what sets them off.

Psychiatrists delve into these things in search of what triggers this behavior, and most are quite good at coming up with solutions to the patient's problems. But first they have to get to know their patient and discover the root cause of a problem in order to deal with it intelligently. Sound familiar?

You're probably not a psychiatrist or psychologist and I know I'm not. But the principle is the same.

"The better you get to know your students, the better they get to know you, the better they behave."

If you put this one principle into practice, you will see behavior problems in your school and classrooms go down significantly.

> There are a variety of ways to handle disruptive students. It depends on a variety of variables including their personality, intelligence level, environment, and culture. Learning styles (auditory, visual, and kinesthetic) also greatly impact the alternative education classroom (including behavior and curriculum).

There are some who are going to have to hear very clearly, in matter-of-fact terms, what the parameters are. There are others where we are simply requesting: Here's what I am trying to do. I really need your help. You do this in a private conversation.

Some will respond if you publicly confront them and some will respond if you take them aside and demonstrate in a respectful manner that you are trying to work with them and you don't want to "highlight" them in front of everybody else.

There is no magical answer. It is why, in my opinion, what is being taught as behavioral management doesn't always work. I think some of the teachers I have hired and seen in action over the years try to cram every student into the same discipline and structure mold.

It doesn't work that way. Teachers have to be innovative and they have got to be willing to reach students in different methodologies and different aspects, even if some ways are foreign or opposite of what the teacher really wants to do.

All we can do is provide a healthy, nurturing environment that is going to challenge them and, if they want, help give them the skills necessary to be successful.

There has got to be a menu. If something happens, here are 17 different options that are available, and there are only 17 because we have not thought of options 18 and 19 and 20. (Dr. Laidacker)

Why do kids seek attention? Why do you and I seek attention? Most likely, it makes us feel special. It sets us apart from the others, at least for a little while. It says, "Here I am! I'm somebody!"

When kids feel they can't compete with other students, academically or athletically, or even in popularity, they at times get the urge to act out. It's their way of competing with other students on their own terms. Sometimes doing inappropriate things in school and in classrooms is the only means they feel they have to "compete."

A grade school kid drops a book on the floor when no one is looking to get some attention. That same student in middle school drops a book and gets some other kid to do the same thing. It makes twice the noise!

What the first kid did not only was attention-getting but also progressed into the influencing stage. It's actually a sign of a student maturing. Attention-getting stuff is no longer satisfying in itself. Now the kid wants and needs to involve other kids into "performing" for the rest of the class.

Think about this. When a stranger pulls over his car and yells out, "Hey, how do I get to Town Hall?" we beam when we know the directions and gleefully offer them to him. That's having influence over someone.

The question is why do students have the need to seek negative attention to the point of getting others to seek that same inappropriate behavior? They probably have concluded that it's the only way they are going to get any attention at all.

When kids feel left out, when they feel they just don't fit in, when they feel lost in class because they have fallen behind the rest of kids academically or any other way, they only have three options:

1. Stay in school, remain quiet, put their time in, and painfully endure the day.
2. Cut school on a regular basis until they drop out because school no longer holds any allure for them.
3. Stay in school and disrupt the educational process on a regular basis.

Numbers 2 and 3 are your most likely candidates for alternative education. They are attention-getting and influencing wrapped up into a neat package. One of my principles is to take whatever is causing the poor behavior out of the equation.

How you proceed with any student in your alternative education program from here on out will require a team approach with each one of these kids. All their problems may have similarities or they may be as different as night and day. But none will be exactly alike. Some kids may be so beaten down they've given up.

Find the problem, isolate it, and find a way to take whatever is causing it out of the equation. It may be as simple as teaching students how to study for a test that will produce the best results. It may be something totally unrelated to school.

Attention-getting always has a reason attached to it. Influencing others to misbehave in class is attention-getting taken to a higher level. Deal with it as soon as these students get into your school! It should have been dealt with and corrected before this, but for whatever reason, it wasn't! If you don't deal with it quickly, it will escalate and disrupt your program.

> If you look at the 5 stages of group development (which includes classroom development): forming, storming, norming, performing, and transforming, testing the boundaries always occurs immediately after the forming stage. That's the storming stage.
> So whatever is left unclear by the adults determines the "tests" the kid throws out. If the adults do not respond in a way that is effective, the students will continue to test and they will broaden how they test. (Dr. Laidacker)

LIMBO STICKS, ENTITLEMENT, AND ESCAPE

When schools or nations lower the bar to achieve a desired outcome, does anybody really believe they are doing anyone any good? Apparently someone in authority does, because the bar we use to gauge "academic achievement" today reminds me of one of those limbo sticks from yesteryear where the participant shuffled low and slow to scoot under the bar, which is only two feet off the floor.

If we took that same limbo stick today and placed it that same two feet off the floor, the goal would be to leap over it! Lowering the bar for academics cheapens achievement. And it creates all kinds of behavioral problems for schools. Kids already have the mistaken belief they have the right to an education. They don't. They have a right to an opportunity to have an education.

Some kids today actually believe they don't have to put any effort into school in order to pass and advance up the ladder. They think somebody somewhere will see to it they don't flunk a subject or flunk out of school. When kids are brought up with this mind-set, what stops them from acting out with impunity? This entitlement we have bestowed upon these kids is one of the main reasons there is so much inappropriate behavior in schools.

I once read that entitlement not only is the opposite of achievement but also undermines incentive to do all the hard work that leads to achievement. Whoever said this was right on the mark.

Understand the mind-set of kids who may be gracing your alternative school. Don't fault them for it. Sometimes they have been brought up to think this way.

> What I have seen is that some of those at the top of the food chain don't understand alternative education in this aspect. The grades and the testing do not matter if the behaviors don't match. So the most important thing is to have impact on the behaviors. Once the behaviors have been straightened out, then it is possible to work on the quantitative stuff.
>
> But in this country, with all of our slogans like 3 strikes you're out or zero tolerance, or laws in place like No Child Left Behind, what often ends up happening is we worry about the numbers games, we worry about the test scores, and we lose sight of and don't care about the behavior.
>
> If we don't get the behavior, you're not going to get the desired test result. But we are not allowed to work on the behaviors. Instead, in elementary school we far too frequently use medication so by the time they become alternative education students their behavior has often never effectively been dealt with.
>
> And so, it routinely negatively impacts grades and with today's pressure on grades and numbers we lose focus on the behavior. If the behavior is managed then the grades and numbers improve. It seems to be an ass-backwards system. (Dr. Laidacker)

When all else fails, zap them! Some kids even medicate themselves on a regular basis. Do you have any idea how many of your students will have ingested illegal narcotics before they arrive in your alternative school? I can assure you, the percentage is higher than you expect.

When life becomes painful, some of these kids turn to drugs and alcohol for a quick escape. Keep your eyes and ears open and be attuned to the signs of chemical abuse. If a student is using, it may answer some of your questions as to why you can't get through to this kid.

Alcohol, marijuana, and harder drugs are an easy way for these kids to build a wall around themselves. These things are readily available, addicting, and very attractive to a student who is struggling with life and school and needs an escape. Ask your school nurse or some other qualified professional for guidance in spotting this scourge in today's schools.

But think about it. We are guilty of drugging some of these kids when we give up on dealing with the underlying problems causing their disruptive behavior. Make no mistake, behavioral disorders are very real. But we have swung the pendulum so far the other way that "prescription" solutions have become the norm rather than the exception. It is easier to medicate than take the time to rehabilitate behavior. Just like it is easier to lower the bar than adhere to a higher standard.

> In many instances a student gets a free or reduced meal plan, so we give them something to eat in the morning. Typically, we fill them with starch. Donuts, toast, bagels, and cereals, for example. Then at lunch time, French fries and a burger in a bun. More starch (sugar).
> They already have difficulty sitting still and focusing and paying attention. We fill them with sugar and ask them to sit still for blocks of time. When they demonstrate that they cannot sit still and focus, we give them psychotropic meds to slow them down (Ritalin and Adderall) for ADHD, conduct disorder, impulse control issues, etc.
> Unfortunately, public education has become a system rather than individualized. In special education we talk about individualized programs all the time, but with the kids who may also need individualization it kind of falls on deaf ears. (Dr. Laidacker)

It is a reality of alternative schools that most of the students assigned for specific periods of time will be mainstreamed back into regular education classes. Some, of course, will remain in your program for longer periods of time or for the duration of their school days. That is to be expected and should not alarm anyone.

Some kids just don't fit into the regular school setting. It doesn't mean they aren't intelligent enough to do the work; it may be that they never felt comfortable being surrounded by hundreds of other kids on a daily basis or having to deal with teachers who don't understand who they are and what they are going through in their lives. As one former alternative student put it, "I just don't need all the mad drama over there."

You will have students who have found a "home" in your alternative school. They are more relaxed, put forth a better effort on a daily basis, and attend regularly. If this is the case, if this is where they and their schoolwork are prospering, allow them to remain. This is a desirable outcome.

When students go back and forth between regular and alternative education like a boomerang, it may be an indication they are trying to get back to where they feel safer. However, if students try to get back into the alternative program by continually disrupting regular education classes, it may be they think your program has become so lax with discipline and work requirements that it is an easy way out.

Of course this is not desirable. It teaches a child a terrible lesson: act out enough times and you will be returned to what they consider "easy street." Don't fall into this trap. These types of students probably pull this same stunt at home with remarkable consistency and success. You are not doing them any favors by giving in to them so they are not "subjected" to the same standards as other regular education students.

This is another reason you must have a small staff of trained and experienced faculty who can spot this type of thing and make an intelligent call as to where any student should be.

Therefore it is imperative to receive progress reports when an alternative student is returned to regular education, if nothing more than to see if the strategies you employed to straighten out this kid and get him back on track are working. If you don't, you are missing a great opportunity for feedback, which is vital for any institution to gauge success, or to identify failed methodology that needs correction.

> If the regular education system doesn't understand this student population and refuses to make the adjustments that are necessary to deal with these kids, then there are going to be students who find safety and value in an alternative setting. So there may be students who spend three or four years in alternative education and graduate from there.
>
> But it is important to have recidivism data. It's important to generate a system. For students who return to regular education, the school may need to know how many days they attended school. What kind of grades they are getting. If they have any disciplinary actions. Are they employed? Are they going to school?
>
> Create a database to make determinations. Don't make decisions anecdotally. Then future programming decisions can be based on true data and results. (Dr. Laidacker)

Expectations in an alternative school can be a double-edged sword. It's important you have expectations and it's important the students assigned to your program understand in this school, as in life, rules are going to be put in place for the safety and well-being of everyone.

The other side of that sword is some of these kids have never followed any rules and are not about to start in your "stinking" school! So the expectations that you are attempting to apply to them will be met with scorn and ridicule. That's all right. It's to be expected.

Be cautious when instituting rules that are just plain unenforceable. Or, if they are enforceable, consume so much time and generate such bad will between your faculty and the student population they do more harm than good. Only with experience and common sense will you come up with a plan of conduct that is doable and acceptable to your faculty but that also seems fair and reasonable to the students.

Keep in mind, this is your place. When you let students and parents dictate what goes on in your alternative program, you're done! This also, by the way, applies to regular education.

For all these reasons, it is a horrible idea for administrators to dictate to the faculty what the rules and expectations will be for your alternative program. First, they are rarely on the premises to be able to make any kind of rational, informed call. And secondly, it is insulting to the staff that is trying to work with these kids to not be consulted on these matters for their input.

James Baker, an American attorney, politician, and political advisor, once said, "If you're not going to pull the trigger, don't point the gun."

For instance, don't put rules in place that you know are not going to be followed—like nightly homework. It will rarely be started, let alone finished by these kids. In short, if you don't have the commitment, time, or ability to enforce a rule, don't put it in place. Period!

Attempting to enforce the unenforceable is exhausting to everyone concerned and almost always ends up with the faculty on the losing end, which weakens their authority.

This needs repeating here: Sometimes it seems teachers and administrators are on different teams. When they are, your program in all likelihood is heading toward failure.

> First of all, forget the word *rules*. For alternative education kids, and all kids, it's a matter of expectations and that the adults are with them, not against them. When an adult threatens them with something that is unenforceable, it diminishes the program's authority and enhances the student's willingness, and almost need to misbehave. That's the storming stage.
>
> Making kids who may have more emotional and acting out issues than even special education students adhere to the same standards as regular education kids makes little sense.
>
> When administrations pass down their list of rules, I'd suggest that it needs to be demonstrated why some of those things may not be effective, and sometimes impossible with this student population. Make suggestions and then all you can do is kick it back up for consideration. (Dr. Laidacker)

THE REAL WORLD

After dealing with countless thousands of students in regular and alternative education, I have come to the conclusion that poor behavior is directly linked to a misinterpretation and a misunderstanding of how the real world works. You and I would probably have a tainted view of things if we were bombarded, on a daily basis, with mindless video games and songs that devalue life and promote cruelty to our fellow man as some kind of birthright.

Add to that television shows that make rudeness and incivility an acceptable form of entertainment. Then throw in the policies this country has adopted that say kids are not responsible for their behavior because they have been "diagnosed" with this disorder or that disorder.

In one study, more than 70 percent of administrators confessed to treading cautiously when it comes to initiating any type of correction for poor behavior for fear of being sued! Add into the mix some enabling parents or guardians who rarely hold their child accountable for their actions at home, let alone in a school building.

We scratch our heads and wonder why some of these kids make poor choices. All the students you will have in your program have different expectations of life and what it holds for them. Unfortunately, it rarely mirrors the world of reality, and under the circumstance, that is entirely understandable.

A goal-driven alternative school, however, must closely mirror the world these kids are about to enter. When you institute structure and expectations that are designed to make the school a training ground for things they will encounter after they leave school, and they understand that is the reason you have put those very expectations in place, you will find most students on board with it.

As in the workplace, students are expected to be on time, do the assigned tasks for the day, and meet deadlines for those tasks. They are to be respectful to their bosses (teachers) and comply with all the rules put in place for their safety.

A good way to earn the trust of these kids is to have a certain number of breaks (other than lunch) that they may take as they see fit. They are allowed five minutes during a two-hour shift to use the bathroom, get a drink of water, or simply to get up to stretch their legs and get a breath of fresh air, and they may choose when to do that. I suggest they be allowed to take these breaks one at a time. This says to them, "You are a young adult, you have done nothing to cause me to mistrust you, and this is a privilege you have earned by respecting the rules we have put in place."

Understand, not all kids are going to comply with your expectations. They didn't get like this overnight. Don't get mad and don't threaten them with punishment when they break a rule. Sit down with them and explain once again why these rules are put in place and why it is in the best interest of everyone here. Remain calm but demonstrate through your words and demeanor that this is your place and you need them to respect that. If the tables were reversed and you were in their place, you would expect to be held fully accountable for your actions.

Students who believe they matter to you behave far better than students who think they don't.

> The school has to become somewhere where they want to be. Attendance at alternative programs I've been involved with skyrocketed once they realized it was a safe, comfortable place for them to be and they decided they WANTED to be there.
>
> I don't think you entice them to come to school through punishment. I think they determine this is a place they wish to be and that's when things, like attendance, start to improve. It doesn't work for every kid, but I think that's the key to it. (Dr. Laidacker)

All work and no play make Jack a dull boy. Physical activity has been recognized as an integral part of the workday. Some corporations actually set aside time periods for employees to work out in the company gym and even pay for memberships to fitness centers.

It is sound thinking. It relieves stress, promotes healthy lifestyles, produces a more efficient and happy worker, and can just be a whole lot of fun! So where does recreation fit into your alternative program? I can tell you where it doesn't fit in, at the end of the day as some sort of reward.

You are going to have kids in your alternative program who have shunned physical activity at every turn only to come to school and insist that a large portion of their day be spent in the gym! I like their enthusiasm, but often wonder about their motives. Is it because this is the only place they can get some physical activity? Or are they trying to bypass the academic part of your school?

How do you know which is which? When you take them for their scheduled activity, look around to see who is participating and who is sitting or standing around, and you should have your answer.

State mandates usually require alternative schools to mirror the regular education classes in your school. Whatever percentage of the day is supposed to be devoted to math or English or social studies, those percentages are assigned for the alternative program. How much of a school day is required for physical education in regular school should mirror your recreation times.

I suggest dividing these times into two or three segments throughout the day. It breaks up the day and gives the students something to look forward to. However, physical activity is a requirement for physical education classes in regular education and it should be a requirement in your alternative school.

> I believe in the adage, "If you don't wear them out, they are going to wear you out!" I'm a firm believer of exhausting them physically every single day. I don't necessarily view recreation as a reward time but as a necessity for these students to help them deal with ADHD and all their impulsive traits.
>
> It should not be at the end of the day. The stick and carrot thing will work for your general education population, but it is not necessarily going to work with

your difficult kids. My most difficult classes and dormitories need to have major physical activity a couple of times during a course of a day.

Sometimes that can't always work and still meet credit requirements and various educational mandates. But I'm basically a believer if you don't physically exhaust them and work them from their strengths, they are going to be more resistant.

Most of these kids we're talking about don't like being in a classroom because they don't do well there. They can't sit and focus. They do better with physical activity and some sports. Begin intertwining activity and things they are good at with classroom assignments. We can't just continue to force them to do subjects they hate. Maybe disperse to the gym after a real difficult class for some downtime.

It's a different approach that needs to be taken with this student population. (Dr. Laidacker)

STARTING AT HOME

All students' stories begin in the home. It can be a nurturing place or so dysfunctional a child avoids it as much as possible. That is not always the fault of the parents. Some kids, for reasons unknown at times, simply fall in with the wrong crowd and make choices so poor it has this kid's family shaking their heads in disbelief.

But there is always a reason a student ends up in an alternative program. You can do everything in your power as a member of the faculty to right this kid's ship, yet nothing seems to work. Oftentimes, the reason is staring you right in the face.

Each night he goes back to a place where arguing and fighting among family members has become the norm. Each night she goes home to an empty house or, worse, a silent house where communication has broken down.

All the good you have accomplished with this student during the day may be shattered after he leaves the safe confines of your alternative school. When rifts go unmended they grow larger. Until we accept as educators that home and school life are undeniably connected, that one affects the other, for good or bad, we will be fighting a daily uphill battle with some of these students.

During that first interview, the lines of communication should have been opened with the parents. It is preferable that each staff member is present during that interview (although that is not always possible) so the parents know that you are decent and dedicated people and can see you are here not only for their child but for them also.

You need to form a bond with not only their child but also them. And this bond needs to be nurtured throughout their kid's stay in your alternative school. It is in everyone's best interest.

The more often the parents and probation officers can be in the school, the better. Maybe different events, like cookouts, for a couple of hours every two weeks or so. Do different events that bring everyone together.

The more comfortable the parents are, the more comfortable they will be discussing real issues. The more times they can be there when things aren't bad the better. Parents often don't want to be involved because for years all they've heard is how horrible and what a disruptive student he is. (Dr. Laidacker)

Have the parents, the student, and a representative of your alternative school sign two copies of the following "Declaration of Expectations" sheet. You keep one copy, and the parents and student the other.

What We Need You to Understand

We expect you to be on time every day. It's a great habit that builds character and will serve you well for the rest of your life.

We expect you to work hard while you are here for a better tomorrow. Your life and how it turns out is in your hands and your hands only.

We expect you to be honest, especially with yourself. Honesty and a good work ethic will take you further in life than trigonometry and Latin. There, we said it!

We expect you to be a good role model for your little brothers and sisters and the young kids who look up to you and want to be just like you. Don't let them down.

We expect you to take full responsibility for your actions. Quit blaming others for your circumstances. We all have been through some rough times. It doesn't mean your life is over. It sometimes simply means your life must begin again.

We expect you to know we all fail and screw up from time to time. It doesn't just happen to you. Failure is necessary for all of us to grow as human beings. It's a part of life we all experience.

We expect you to know the one thing that can turn anyone's life around quickly is the one thing we all have total control over: our attitude.

We expect you to know you matter to us. We see value in you and want you to have the best life possible. Give us a chance to prove it.

We expect you to know life is not fair; it never has been and never will be, for any of us. Life is what you make of it, for good or bad. That's entirely up to you.

We expect you to stop complaining when things don't go your way. A level playing field is nothing more than a myth. Sometimes other students get ahead for the simplest of reasons; they want it more and are willing to put in the time and effort to make their dreams come true. You can do that, too. We'll show you how to get started.

Finally, we expect you to know we, the teachers, are here to help you. It's not only why we're here but also why we want to be here. Before you write us off, give us the same chance we are giving to you.

This chapter should not only provide a blueprint for a successful alternative education program but should also give you the information necessary to answer the three questions listed in the beginning of the chapter.

Appendix 1

In a Nutshell . . .

- Know your audience. Make it a priority early on. The better you know your students, the better they behave. This is especially true for disruptive students. Kids of any age want to know they matter. Just making an effort to get to know them, their likes and dislikes, says "you matter to me."
- If you want respect, give respect. Always deal with every situation with class and poise. Set an example for the entire class about how mature people respond. When you demonstrate respect in trying moments, you are giving them a valuable life lesson.
- Let them save face. Disruptive kids are oftentimes being who they think they need to be in order to survive or fit in. Take the "necessary" out of their thinking. Never correct them in front of their peers. Never attempt to correct them while they're agitated. And never, ever talk down to them! Always talk to them.
- Let them correct themselves. When you make the effort to correct a student, it sometimes fails. It's not sustainable. When students are permitted to correct themselves, with your help, it makes a lasting impression. It says to them, "This was my decision. I was wrong. I own up to it. Thanks for not jumping down my throat!"
- Address unwanted behavior immediately. Small messes are easier to clean up than big messes. Poor behavior left unaddressed almost always escalates.
- Let them buy into you. About 95 percent of teaching is your relationship with your students. The other 5 percent is paperwork. You must be someone they want to look up to. They must buy into you before they buy into what you're selling. Kids influence other kids' behavior, for good or bad. When an entire class perceives you to be a decent person, disruptive students usually fall in line in order to fit in.

- Don't let it go to your head. Disruptive students oftentimes have the perception, whether real or imagined, that you think you're better than them, talking down and never giving them their "props." Remember: it's about them, not you.
- Take whatever is causing the unwanted behavior out of the equation. When you're so rigid, so inflexible, so uncompromising, some students pick up on it and rebel. Each class has a different set of characters. You may need a different approach some periods. Some kids need a pat on the head; some kids need a kick in the pants. Learn to change the environment, not the student.
- You're the only adult in the room, so act like one! Even your most disruptive student fully expects you to be in charge. They're disruptive, not stupid! Your students are just waiting for you to "step up" and claim your territory. When you hesitate, or are indecisive, they claim it. Your classroom is not a democracy. It's a benevolent dictatorship.
- Don't prejudge. Don't allow someone else's opinion to influence you. Kids pick up on negative vibes and oftentimes base their behavior on them. Always give each student a clean slate at the start of the semester *and* after a correction. Once you have the reputation as one who is tough but fair, word gets around. Now, the ball is in their court. If they muck it up, it's their fault, and they know it!
- Never forget this one basic fact: *all kids are basically good kids.*

Appendix 2

Your Life, Your Call . . .

The students who have an "in your face, up yours" attitude usually have a distorted view of the world and how it actually works. The constant exposure to corrupting influences like TV shows that depict vulgar behavior acceptable to this aura of invincibility that they think swirls around them makes them more brazen and willing to challenge authority.

What they fail to appreciate is that our twenty-first-century world is so interconnected, fast-paced, and competitive that it will, by its very nature, leave behind those who don't prepare for it or refuse to take it seriously. For many reasons, they feel it's necessary to act the fool and disrupt the educational process.

The following is a frank talk with these kids in an attempt to take the "necessary" out of their thinking in order to put them on the road to recovery. It is a small capsule of my program geared to the students themselves.

I once asked a classroom full of students, "What's the worst thing about school?" And from the back of the room came a loud reply that nearly all the other students seemed to agree with, since all their heads were bobbing up and down in unison: "It sucks!"

They were a little stunned when I said, "I agree! And I'm going to let you all in on little secret that most teachers won't share with you, but I will: it sucks for us sometimes!"

The rest of the talk went a little something like this:

I mean, is school *really* necessary? Everybody keeps telling all of you, "You need a good education to get ahead in this dangerous, competitive world," and my question is, "Why?"

I know of people who quit school and are still quite wealthy. And I know people who are really smart but don't have a lick of common sense. They get straight As in school, but if you put a chicken and a rabbit in front of them and ask them to point out the chicken, they'd scratch their heads and have trouble making up their minds.

We all know people who fit neatly into one of these groups. So back to my original question, "Is school really necessary?" Is a good education really all that it's cracked up to be? Or is it overrated and maybe a total crock? Are we educators being honest with you when we keep pounding into your heads that without a good education your chances of making it in this world are not real good?

I'm going to try and answer all these questions for you as honestly as I know how. I've been around literally thousands of students over the years and know first-hand what some of you are going through, why some of you aren't doing well in school and would dearly love to walk out of here and never look back.

Some of you come from homes so broken, every day is a struggle just to get out of bed, let alone come to school. Some of you are depressed and the answers you're looking for are definitely not in this place, so you avoid school as much as possible or just shut down when you're here. You just don't fit in, you feel out of place, you're being bullied or threatened, and you don't know what to do about it. Everybody you've confided in has been little or no help. You've fallen so far behind that each period might as well be taught in Greek, because you don't understand that either and you're starting to feel really dumb, lashing out at anybody who starts to pile on. You're mad, and you're not going to take it anymore. You can't take it anymore. Anything is better than this. You just want to get away from it all.

You cover up all this pain and disillusionment with life and school by lying to yourself and everyone else that you don't need this garbage! All this school stuff is useless and anybody who studies hard and thinks that will get them ahead is a fool, a nerd, and a geek. You resent them because they have gotten all the breaks in life and think they're better than you, and they deserve to be brought down a peg or two, and by God, you and your buddies are just the ones to do it.

Some of you are getting absolutely no encouragement to try harder, or are being pushed so much and compared to everyone else that you have thrown up your hands and said, "Enough!" No matter what you do or how hard you try, it's never enough, so who cares anymore? And some of you are so smart that school presents no challenge so you look for other things to keep your interest. And in some districts, kids avoid school because they fear for their very lives. They either join the ones who are wreaking havoc in school or avoid it altogether. It gets old being scared all the time, so what other choice do you have?

I've seen it all, and I not only understand what you're going through but can also empathize with you. You've got to do what you've got to do, even though you know it doesn't make sense because anyone in their right mind knows it's a dead end leading to nowhere. Some students I've dealt with were going through some terrible times in their lives—things that would overwhelm and crush another student—and they were forced to deal with it on a daily basis as best they could. So they lashed out and disrupted class on a daily basis, too. I get that, because I've seen it too many times to ignore.

And then, of course, there are the handful of students who don't want to come to school because they think they know it all already, and when they do grace us with their presence, all they want to do is act like jerks all day long, which I'll be the first to admit can be a whole lot of fun, but never accomplishes anything other than to screw you and everybody else over, which is really dumb.

Life is all about choices, and whether you stay in school and get as much out of it as you can, or you quit, is going to be one of those choices you'll have to make. Nobody has the right to judge your decision, and I promise you, I won't do that! It's your life, and it must be your choice.

What I'm going to do today is show you where those choices in all probability are leading you. Since looking ahead is not most young people's strongest suit, I'm going to look ahead for you. You don't get to be my age without figuring out how to not only survive it but also thrive in it. You learn through trial and error as you go through life. You learn from your mistakes so you don't repeat them, I hope. Some people, for whatever reason, never seem to learn that doing the same dumb thing over and over never gets you anywhere. I'm positive some names just popped into your head. Maybe your own.

The real world can be fun and challenging, with endless possibilities; the sky's the limit for those who take it seriously and prepare for it. But it can be a very scary, stressful place for those who don't prepare for it, because it can eat you up and spit you out so fast you wouldn't even know what hit you. If you don't believe me, take a look around at the people who decided not to prepare for life when they were your age. Better yet, ask them what it's like. Ask them if they wished they would have put a little more effort into this preparedness stuff when they were your age. Ask them, if they could do it all over again, would they do anything different? I know some of you won't ask anyone those questions because you already know the answer, and it frightens you, and it should.

About 90 percent of the students who quit school are living in poverty by the age of twenty-five. About 50 percent of the prison populations in this country are high school dropouts! That alone should be a wake-up call for some of you!

The one question that drove me relentlessly for years was actually quite simple: Why do some people choose to fail? Do you realize that out of all the species that inhabit our planet, only one, when given a choice between success and failure, oftentimes chooses failure? That's us. Human beings. And I had to ask, "Why?" Why do some people—in this case students—prefer to fail at life, be miserable, and always struggle to get from here to there? Why do some students put themselves in the position of living hand to mouth for the rest of their lives, depending on other people to look after them, all the time complaining about how hard life is and how unfair it is that some people seem to have it all, and they have nothing? The other guy always seems to have the well-paying job, and they're stuck with whatever is left over.

The other guy lives in a nice house, drives a nice car, always living large, taking nice vacations and wearing nice clothes, and they're left behind just trying to make ends meet. Every day is the same, boring and getting worse, with little or no prospects for a better future or a better life for them and their kids.

Listen closely. This may be the most important thing I say here today. And for those of you who fall into the category of wanting to drop out, for whatever reason, or stick around and just take up space, or always take it a step further and disrupt class every chance you get because you have this overwhelming need to play the fool all day long, listen especially close:

The vast majority of poverty in this country is self-inflicted! Let me repeat that so there is no mistaking what I just said: *The vast majority of poverty in this country is self-inflicted!*

And I'm not only talking about having no money. I'm talking about unhappiness, discontentment with life, and the stress that comes with it. And maybe the biggest poverty of all, *hopelessness*. If someone forced you into the life some of you are barreling toward at breakneck speed, you'd be mad, and you'd have every right to be. You'd say, "What? Are you crazy? Nobody in their right mind would choose to live like that!"

And yet, here some of you are, doing everything in your power to make sure that's exactly the type of life you have. Does that make any sense to anyone?

I want you to ask yourself one question right now. How you answer it will pretty much tell you all you need to know about how your future's going to play out: Am I willing to settle for what I'm becoming, or do I want more out of life?

Your answer should give you a clear picture of what the next fifty to sixty years will look like. If you don't like the picture rattling around your head, it's time to do something about it, *now*! Nothing changes if nothing changes! You keep on doing what you're doing and you'll keep on getting what you got.

But I'm not here to tell you what to do with your life. That's up to you. I'm going to show you how your future will probably play out, give you some odds, and let you decide if you want to keep going down that road you're on. I've been around a long time and I'm supposed to know more than you about how this world works, where the pitfalls are, where the opportunities can be found, and I'm going to share those with you. It doesn't mean I'm smarter than you, just that I have more experience, and experience is precisely what young people lack.

School's not for everybody, and it sucks at times! I get that, because at one time I was sitting right where you are sitting. Never forget that!

A former student of ours who had dropped out for two years asked to come back to school. His goal was to graduate by his twenty-first birthday. I asked him, "Why did you want to come back?"

"It's really tough out there without an education. There's just nothing worthwhile without a diploma."

Then he looked around the room at all the other wannabe dropouts and kids who were constantly whining about how school was a waste of time and said, "I could just shake some of these kids, they have no idea what it's like out there."

I'm going to tell you what it's like out there. Then you're going to have a decision to make. Choose wisely; your future depends on it.

References and Resources

BEHAVIOR MANAGEMENT/MOTIVATION

Social psychologists Leon Festinger and J. Merrill Carlsmith espoused a theory of cognitive dissonance, which is the feeling of uncomfortable tension that comes from holding two conflicting thoughts in mind at the same time. Dissonance increases with the importance of the subject to us, how strongly the dissonant thoughts conflict, and our inability to rationalize and explain away the conflict. Cognitive dissonance is a powerful motivator that often creates a tension that leads us to take one of three actions: change our behavior, justify our behavior by changing the conflicting cognition, or justify our behavior by added new cognitions. *Source:* ChangingMinds.org

Kathryn R. Wentzel in the Department of Human Development at the University of Maryland, in her study, "Motivating Students to Behave in Socially Competent Ways," published in the Autumn 2003 issue of *Theory into Practice*, says a caring classroom environment in which teachers and peers support and promote the expression of positive social behaviors appears to play a critical role in promoting students' adoption and pursuit of positive social goals. This model also highlights the importance of the classroom social ecology in promoting a student's sense of belongingness, and thus, motivation to engage in appropriate classroom behavior.

According to Ramon Lewis, director of graduate research in the School of Education Studies at La Trobe University, Victoria, Australia, in *Understanding Pupil Behavior: Classroom Management Techniques for Teachers*, published in 2008 by ACER Press, an imprint of Australian Council for Educational Research, "Many of these difficult kids believe the teacher is playing the man and not the ball and the data from the study supports that. If any teacher gives them any hint of dislike or rejection they're very likely to pick up on that and their behavior worsens. It's important for teachers locked in this spiral to recognize that the only behavior they can control is their own. If they can do that then the child is more likely to cooperate."

Lewis found that teacher aggression, such as yelling angrily, and the use of punishments, such as class detention, were ineffective in fostering good, responsible behavior among students. He also contends that in all classroom situations, whether students were badly behaved or not, misbehaving students responded better to more inclusive, less aggressive tactics from teachers.

COGNITIVE DEVELOPMENT

Russian psychologist Lev Vygotsky asserted that social interaction plays a fundamental role in the process of cognitive development and in fact precedes cognitive development. He also discussed the zone of proximal development (ZPD), which is the distance between a student's ability to perform a task under adult guidance and/or with peer collaboration and the student's ability to solve the problem independently. According to Vygotsky, learning occurs in this zone. *Source:* Learning-Theories.com

James Marcia, emeritus professor of psychology at Simon Fraser University, British Colombia, argues that two distinct parts form an adolescent's identity: crisis (i.e., a time when one's values and choices are being reevaluated) and commitment. He defined a crisis as a time of upheaval when old values or choices are being reexamined. The end outcome of a crisis leads to a commitment made to a certain role or value. He contends in "Development and Validation of Ego Identity Status," published in the 1966 *Journal of Personality and Social Psychology*, volume 3, that one's sense of identity is determined largely by choices and commitments made regarding certain personal and social traits.

Albert Bandura, professor emeritus of social science in psychology at Stanford University, posits that people learn from one another via observation, imitation, and modeling. People learn through observing others' behavior, attitudes, and outcomes of those behaviors. He states in *Social Learning Theory*, published in 1977 by Prentice Hall: "Most human behavior is learned observationally through modeling: from observing others, one forms an idea of how new behaviors are performed, and on later occasions, this coded information serves as a guide for action."

John B. Watson, Ivan Pavlov, B. F. Skinner, E. L. Thorndike, Albert Bandura, and Edward Tolman are the founders of behaviorism, which operates on a principle of "stimulus-response." Behaviorism is a worldview that assumes a learner is essentially passive, responding to environmental stimuli. The learner starts as a clean slate and behavior is shaped through positive and negative reinforcement. Learning is defined as a change in the behavior in the learner. *Source:* Learning-Theories.com

American psychoanalyst Erik Erikson established an eight-stage theory of identity and psychosocial development. Erikson, heavily influenced by Sigmund Freud, explored three aspects of identity: the ego identity (self), personal identity (the personal idiosyncrasies that distinguish a person from another), and social/cultural identity (the collection of social roles a person might play). His psychosocial theory of development considers the impact of external factors, parents, and society on personality development from childhood to adulthood. *Source:* Learning-Theories.com

Bernard Weiner in the Department of Psychology at UCLA promotes an attribution theory that assumes that people try to determine why people do what they do. A three-stage process underlies an attribution: (1) Behavior must be observed/perceived. (2) Behavior must be determined to be intentional. (3) Behavior is attributed to internal or external causes. *Source:* Learning-Theories.com

Abraham Maslow, Carl Rogers, and Malcolm Knowles are key proponents of humanism, a paradigm/philosophy pedagogical approach that views learning as a personal act to fulfill one's potential. The central assumption is that people act with intentionality and values. Humanists believe that it is necessary to study the person as a whole, especially as an individual grows and develops over a lifespan. In humanism, learning is student centered and personalized, and the educator's role is that of a facilitator. Affective and cognitive needs are key, and the goal is to develop self-actualized people in a cooperative, supportive environment. *Source:* Learning-Theories.com

Jerome Bruner, American psychologist and senior research fellow at New York University, contends that learning is an active process in which learners construct new ideas or concepts based on their current/past knowledge. Cognitive structures (i.e., schema, mental models) provide meaning and organization to experiences and allow the individual to go beyond the information given. The task of the instructor is to translate information to be learned into a format appropriate to the learner's current state of understanding. Curriculum should be organized in a spiral manner so that the student continually builds upon what they have already learned. *Source:* Learning-Theories.com

Dr. John Keller at Florida State University identifies, in his ARCS Model of Motivational Design, four steps for promoting and sustaining motivation in the learning process: attention, relevance, confidence, and satisfaction. According to Keller, learning must be rewarding or satisfying in some way, whether it is from a sense of achievement, from praise from an educator, or merely providing entertainment. *Source:* Learning-Theories.com

RELATIONSHIPS

Jesse Sackett and Ho Chun, in their 1998 study "How Are Classroom Behaviors of Students with Chronic Behavior Problems Related to their Perceptions of Teacher 'Coolness'?" posit that in order to be perceived as "cool" by a student, and thus experience fewer behavior problems, it is important for teachers to develop a positive, close relationship with students, and to show the students that they are cared about.

Christi Bergin at the University of Maryland and David Bergin at the University of Missouri published an article titled, "Attachment in the Classroom," in the May 2009 issue of *Educational Psychology Review*. In abstract, attachment influences students' school success. This is true of students' attachment to their parents as well as their teachers.

Secure attachment is associated with higher grades and standardized test scores. Secure attachment also is associated with greater emotional regulation, social competence, willingness to take on challenges, and lower levels of ADHD and delinquency, each of which in turn is associated with higher achievement. These effects tend to be stronger for high-risk students. *Source:* Cengage Learning

James Neill at the Centre for Applied Psychology, University of Canberra, Australia, summarized John Dewey's findings in his book *Experience and Education*, published by MacMillan. According to Dewey, a good education should have both a societal purpose and a purpose for the individual student. For Dewey, the long-term matters, but so does the short-term quality of an educational experience. Educators are responsible, therefore, for providing students with experiences that are immediately valuable and that better enable the students to contribute to society. Dewey criticized the traditional education for lacking in holistic understanding of students and designing curricula overly focused on content rather than content and process which is judged by its contribution to the well-being of individuals and society.

Social and behavioral scientist Tim Mainhard, from Utrecht University in the Netherlands, contends that the relationship between a teacher and class is important for the learning achievement of pupils and their pleasure in learning, and can remain stable over the course of a school year. Consequently, if teachers get off to a bad start, it is almost impossible to put things right. He advises in his November 4, 2009, *Science Daily* article that teachers to try to build up a relationship with a class from the outset that is characterized by a large degree of influence and proximity, and notes that a single poor lesson does not mean the rest of the school year is lost. In addition, he advises against frequent use of coercion and sanctions in class. Besides causing clear and immediate damage to the relationship with the class, such measures do nothing to increase the teacher's influence in the class.

The Active Listening Training Program on Intractable Conflict from the Conflict Research Consortium at the University of Colorado posits that active listening improves mutual understanding. It forces people to listen attentively to others; it avoids misunderstandings, as people have to confirm that they do really understand what the other person has said; and it tends to open people up, to get them to say more. If people believe their opponent is really attuned to their concerns and wants to listen, they are likely to explain in detail what they feel and why. If both parties to a conflict do this, the chances of developing a solution increase.

Melissa Maki, research communications coordinator at the University of Virginia, reports in "Student-Teacher Relationships Key to Cooperative Classrooms," published in the November 24, 2008, issue of *USA Today*, that disruptive and defiant behavior within the classroom is a common reason for high school student suspension. Such outbursts can negatively affect student learning and increase teacher stress. Moreover, students who have been suspended are at a higher risk of dropping out of high school and committing crimes.

Anne Gregory, of the Curry School of Education's Programs in Clinical and School Psychology at the University of Virginia, in a study with doctoral student Michael Ripski, found that building student-teacher relationships may be the key to preventing trouble in the classroom. In their Fall 2008 *School Psychology Review* article, "Adolescent Trust in Teachers: Implications for Behavior in the High School Classroom," they report that students who had been suspended were more cooperative in classes where teachers took a relational approach to discipline—that is, they consciously worked to prevent classroom conflict through relationship building.

Diana Baumrind, clinical and developmental psychologist at the Institute of Human Development, University of California at Berkeley, and Eleanor Maccoby, in the Department of Psychology at Stanford University, theorize that some children raised in dramatically different environments can later grow up to have remarkably similar personalities. Conversely, children who share a home and are raised in the same environment can grow up to have astonishingly different personalities than one another. Despite these challenges, Baumrind suggests that the majority of parents display one of three different parenting styles. Psychologists E. E. Maccoby and J. A. Martin suggest a fourth parenting style in "Socialization in the Context of the Family: Parent-Child Interaction," published in 1983 in *The Handbook of Child Psychology*:

1. Authoritarian Parenting: children are expected to follow strict rules established by parents.
2. Authoritative Parenting: more democratic than authoritarian, children are expected to follow rules and guidelines.

3. Permissive Parenting: sometimes referred to as indulgent parents, have very few demands to make on their children.
4. Uninvolved Parenting: characterized by few demands, low responsiveness, and little communication.

Carol Dweck, Lewis and Virginia Eaton Professor of Psychology at Stanford University, is recognized as one of the world's leading researchers in the field of motivation. Her theories, detailed in *Self-Theories: Their Role in Motivation, Personality, and Development*, published in 1999 by the Psychology Press, reveal why some students are motivated to work harder and why others fall into patterns of helplessness and are self-defeating. She demonstrated empirically that some students have a high desire to prove themselves to others, to be seen as smart and avoid looking unintelligent. Thus, they are less likely to attempt challenging tasks, are at risk of academic underachievement, and are susceptible to learned helplessness because they may feel that circumstances are outside their control and thus give up easily. Or they may purposely choose extremely difficult tasks so they have an excuse for failure.

RECOMMENDED READING

Teacher Man (2005), Frank McCourt, Scribner, 1230 Avenue of the Americas, NY.
The collection of articles by Mary Beth Hewitt, independent educational consultant, featured in Choices Newsletter Articles, Volume 1 & 2, and Reclaiming Children and Youth Magazine.